J. R. Simplot

A billion the hard way

J. R. Simplot
A billion the hard way

Louie Attebery

Caxton Press
Caldwell, Idaho
2001

First printing, October 2000
Second printing, January 2001

Library of Congress Cataloging-in-Publication Data

Attebery, Louie W. (Louie Wayne), 1927-
J. R. Simplot : A billion the hard way / Louie Attebery
p. cm.
Includes bibliographical references and index.
ISBN 0-87004-399-4
1. Simplot, J. R. (John Richard), 1909- 2. J.R. Simplot Company--History. 3. Businessmen--United States--Biography. 4. Food industry and trade--United States--History. I. Title
HD9010.S56 A88 2000
338.7'664'0092--dc21
[B]

00-056970

Lithographed and bound in the United States of America
CAXTON PRESS
Caldwell, Idaho
167007

Dedication

To the memory of my parents, Thomas Attebery, country schoolmaster, teamster, and stockman-farmer who paid off our mortgage during the Depression; Tressie Blevins Attebery Miller, who came from Missouri to Idaho in 1916 and never lost her love for old-time music; and to my brother Jim, who pointed the way to college by precept and example; and to my sister Lois Aspitarte, who in the absence of school buses, put herself through high school by housekeeping in town for board and room, worked for the State of Idaho, bought football shoes for me and supported me as a ninth and tenth grader when I was translated from a country school with eight pupils to the magisterial Boise Junior High School with 1400. Lois served her country with honor as a WAVE in World War II.

CONTENTS

Acknowledgements xiii
Preface xv

1 Antecedents 7
2 The westward migration .13
3 Roots 27
4 The break . . . the making of a venture capitalist . . .43
5 Certified seed 57
6 Courtship and marriage .75
7 The 1940s: War and growth 83
8 The postwar period: Redefining the market 117
9 The 1950s: Expansion 141
10 The Simplot family 149
11 Passing the reins: Growth in the '70s and '80s 165
12 From the heights 201
13 Sands at Ninety 217
14 Afterword 233

The Author 239
Bibliography 241
Index 245

Illustrations

Simplot family tree xxxii
Richard Bonson 97
Elizabeth Nelson 97
Cornelius and Jane Nelson Haxby 97
Charles LeClere Simplot 98
Susan Le Clere Simplot .98
Dorothy Bradley Haxby 98
Mary Bonson Simplot 98
Charles Richard Simplot, age 12 99
Doroty Haxby Simplot, age 12 or 13 99
Charles Richard and Dorothy Haxby Simplot 99
Dick Simplot and friends 100
First Idaho home 100
Dorothy Simplot and children 101
Burley, Idaho, 1912 101
The Simplot kids cool off 102
Jack and the Baker Boys 102
Santa Rosa class photo 103
Simplot "ranch" at Santa Rosa 104
Simplot kids at Santa Rosa home 104
Dick and Jack gather eggs at chicken ranch 105
Simplot kids and the family dog 105
Margaret, Jack and Dick near Eugene, Oregon .106
Jack, Dick and Jack's bum lambs 106
Jack and buddy Marshall Tollman 107
Jack at National Guard summer camp 108
Jack and his big team .109
Jack in Yellowstone Park 109
Dick and Dorothy Simplot in middle age 110
Jack and one of the Enyeart girls 110

Jack and Ruby Simplot about 1930 111
The Simplot family, early 1930s 112
Jack and his first-born, Dick 177
John Sokol, Simplot's first processed food client .177
Simplot's first potato sorter 178
Onion dryer, Caldwell, Idaho, 1941 179
Caldwell plant during the war years 180
Leon Jones 181
R. Starr Farish 181
John Dahl 181
Jack speaks at War Department ceremony 182
Simplot family christmas card, early 1950s 183
Mr. Potato 184
Micron Technology chips and plant 185
Jack and Esther during aerial tour 186
Jack and Tom Basabe, livestock manager 187
Jack with fence painters 187
Phosphate plant, Rock Springs, Wyoming 188
Smoky Canyon Mine, Afton, Wyoming 188
Jack greets a worker 189
Where it all started 189
Simplot home, Boise, Idaho 190
Simplot company logo .191
Jack and Esther Simplot 191
Jack Simplot 192
Louie Attebery 239

Acknowledgements

In the course of the research for this book, much courtesy and many kindnesses were extended to me by many folk, and they deserve thanks.

For guidance through the history of the National Guard in Oregon, I am deeply indebted to Steve McGeorge of the Oregon Military Museum. For copies of the Muster Roll of Jack Simplot's company in the 1926 summer encampment of the Oregon National Guard at Camp Jackson, I extend thanks to the Oregon Secretary of State under whose care the Archives Division, 800 Summer St. NE, Salem, Oregon 97310 is maintained. More particularly, in that division, Dave Wendell did not give up but secured the necessary material for me.

Marilyn Chang of the Western History/Genealogy Department of the Denver Public Library was helpful in pointing me to the right place for finding the Lowell Thomas materials. With her guidance, I discovered Gary Alexander, Director of Denver University's Westminster Law Library, and Paul Sharpe, Access Services Coordinator of that university's College of Law. It is here that the entire collection of radio scripts--from first to last--of Lowell Thomas's newscasts repose in row upon row of thick red volumes, some 544 of them covering fifty-five years.

It was Fred Zerza, Vice President of Public and Government Relations for the J. R. Simplot Company, who called my attention to and later provided me with a copy of Lowell Thomas's remarks on J. R. Simplot, and an examination of the Thomas collection showed that those remarks were not a discrete treatment of Simplot but were part of a longer broadcast. Mr. Zerza patiently fielded many questions, offered helpful suggestions, and served as guide when the way seemed obscure in corporate headquarters.

Dan Knipe shared anecdotes about Mr. Simplot and a truck driver, and Peter Jensen not only kept my eyes functioning but also shared an account of the time he met Jack Simplot while skiing at Bogus Basin.

It was Wayne Cornell, Caxton editor, who asked if I would be interested in tackling a biography of Jack Simplot. For his guidance, encouragement, and professional competence I shall always be grateful.

To Helen (Mrs. Gary) Strine, I owe a debt of immeasurable proportions, for it was she, uncomplaining and reliable, who transcribed the taped sessions with the Simplots and arranged the pedigree chart, from the family research of Margaret Simplot Clayville.

Finally, I thank the crew working for the North Board of Control at Nyssa, Oregon, who, in the summers of 1954 and 1955, spoke endlessly and favorably of the deeds of John Richard Simplot while we kept that great irrigation system functioning.

Preface

Every region has its folk heroes—men and women who because of their accomplishments and/or personalities are viewed by the members of the general population as larger than life. J. R. Simplot is such a modern folk hero. He was brought to Idaho as a months-old baby, grew up along the Snake River, and through hard work, diligence, and the exercise of a quality of imagination that defies analysis gained for himself an international reputation as a self-made billionaire industrialist. This is his story.

What is required to qualify as a modern folk hero? Folk heroes are the central figures—the protagonists—in countless oral narratives. Some of these narratives exist in variant forms. In other words, people tell stories about folk heroes. Some of the stories are true; most have some basis in fact.

With a modest degree of assurance, it may be asserted that most native Idahoans (those who pronounce that name with the accent on the first syllable . . . Idahoans as opposed to IdaHOANS) can tell at least one Jack Simplot story and that many can tell several. He has truly entered the collective consciousness of the state. There is, for instance, the account of the flight over a desirable property.[1]

One day Jack and his pilot were flying from Point A to Point B when Jack saw a piece of ground that looked desirable and instructed his pilot to land the plane and go the house of the landowner to see if he would sell. After complying with his boss's wishes the pilot trudged back to the plane with the news that "You already own it."

Since an item that belongs in the domain of folklore often exists in variant forms, this item qualifies because the following variants have been noted: (1) the pilot is variously identified as Grant Kilbourne, Bob Whipkey, or anonymous; (2) one form has the pilot telling Simplot, "But you already own it" without having to land the plane; (3) the land proves to be for sale, is purchased, becomes highly productive, thus validating the uncanny ability of Simplot to recognize good land even from the air.

Jack Simplot's keen eye for good land is a keystone in the foundation of his success. One of his favorite pieces of advice is "Grab hold of something and hang on!" Over the years Simplot has managed to "hang on" to a lot of real estate. He is the largest private property owner in Idaho, one of the nation's largest states in area. A ranch he owns in central Oregon is 136 miles long and sixty-five miles wide. Simplot, his family and company own 330,000 acres and lease almost two million additional acres. His holdings include more than fifty farms and ranches.

But it takes more than just land to qualify as a folk

hero. A folk hero must perform memorable deeds, too.

During World War II, Jack Simplot's plants produced thirty-three million pounds of dehydrated potatoes and five million pounds of dehydrated onions to fuel America's fighting men and women. In the 1960s, he helped McDonald's chief Ray Kroc turn the french fry into a national staple. In the 1980s, the Idaho farm boy with the eighth grade education played a major role in making the personal computer a household word. And as a new century begins, the company and the man show little sign of resting on their laurels.

Today, Simplot plants produce millions of pounds of potato products annually as well as a variety of other frozen vegetable and meat products. The company ships nearly a half million head of cattle each year. It even raises special cattle (with more fat in the meat) for Japanese consumers. The operation is global, with eleven plants in Australia alone. Simplot phosphate mines produce a sizable chunk of the world's chemical fertilizer, and Simplot Soilbuilders distributes and supplies fertilizer to fields all over the West.

In 1995, *Fortune* magazine listed John Richard Simplot as the thirty-seventh richest American.

But there is another trait that sets Jack Simplot apart from the "average" billionaire and assures his folk hero status. He may live in a fancy house on a hill surrounded by twenty acres of lawn, but he has never lost his rural roots. He has a deep, abiding respect for the people who work for him and genuine interest in their lives—from the division chief to the woman sorting spuds on the french fry line.

How many times in the course of writing this biography, the writer received without solicitation stories of Jack Simplot . . . how he did this, how he said that, what happened when such and such occurred. These narratives are ubiquitous, and their collection would result in a publishable volume. For example:

George, a trucker, was hauling sawdust near a Simplot chicken yard when he was approached by Simplot, who wanted to engage him to haul a large number of truckloads of sawdust for the yard. The trucker told him he had only one truck and couldn't deliver the quantity Simplot wanted but that he could get in touch with another trucker and would arrange to make delivery by a specified date. The cost was agreed upon, Simplot stating that if the material was delivered by that time, he would "take care" of the trucker. The deliveries were made, and George received a check for $500 more than had been agreed to. When the trucker called to inform the Simplot office of the error, he was told, "No, Mr. Simplot said you were to be taken care of because you did what you said you would. That's what the extra money is for."

A farrier was hired by Simplot and charged with the responsibility of keeping the feedlot horses shod. He did his job well, and the demands on his time were few. The feedlot foreman seeing that the farrier appeared to be idle laid some tasks on him. Simplot happened to come by and asked the horseshoer why he was working on the fences. When he was told, Simplot admonished the farrier that he was to keep the horses shod and that was his only job and if that didn't require all his time, well, so be it. But he was working for Simplot as farrier and wasn't to do anything else. To make doubly sure, Simplot repeated the message to the foreman.

Simplot's genuineness comes across to outsiders, too. An acquaintance of the writer put it this way:

"I know some people have said he is a sharp dealer, quick to take advantage and absolutely ruthless. But I met him one time skiing at Bogus Basin, and he didn't know me from Adam. But he was interested in what my name was, and he didn't hesitate to tell me how he used to own the mountain and how he helped it become a ski resort and increase the patronage by enlarging the parking lot. He's a likeable guy."

But not everyone loves a billionaire.

An Idaho native (Idahoan) struck up a conversation during an airplane flight with a woman who had recently moved to the Boise area from another state (IdaHOAN). The conversation turned to Jack Simplot. The woman said she thought it was horrible that under a secret agreement, Boise taxpayers must foot the bill for mowing Simplot's huge lawn. When the woman was told the landscaping duties are handled by a five-person crew paid for by Simplot, she refused to believe it.

In spite of the tendency by writers to enlarge the figure of Jack Simplot (Lowell Thomas described him as "a good-natured giant"[2]), he never magnifies himself, never puts on airs, but like Queequeg in *Moby Dick* is always equal to himself.

That's not to say J. R. Simplot is a humble man. He is proud of what he has accomplished and he loves an opportunity to tell people about his latest project or acquisition. But when Jack Simplot tells someone about his empire in a proud, loud, excited voice, it brings to mind that Muhammad Ali once said, "If you can do what you say, it ain't bragging."

While J. R. Simplot may have his detractors, you won't find many among the thousands of men and women who work for him.

On June 22, 1999, in a twin-engine King Air, two pilots, Jack and Esther Simplot, editor Wayne Cornell, and the biographer flew indirectly from Boise, to Pocatello, to Afton and Rock Springs, Wyoming, to Vernal, Utah, and back to Boise. During the course of this twelve-hour day, unparalleled and unanticipated opportunities appeared, opportunities to view Simplot industries at first hand, to come to a hazy but not inaccurate appreciation of the scale of this man's enterprise through seeing a portion of his phosphate mining-refining activity.

But even more enlightening was the opportunity to observe the human dynamics as the industrialist visited with his hired men and women.

At the Smoky Canyon phosphate mine and mill, a

lunch had been prepared by them for the Simplot party and 200 or more workers. As he walked along the receiving line, Jack visited with each worker, employing his customary language, sprinkled with a "damn" here and a "hell" there—the only language he knows—to talk about the work, about the worker's father who used to work for Jack, about any topic of mutual interest which Jack knew instinctively because he himself had worked with his hands, with machines, and with crews of men. Between employer and worker there was no sense of lord and vassal but something more like reciprocated respect. At times it seemed that the workers were caught up in something like adulation for the man who paid them good wages and upon whose well-being their own welfare depended.

After the employees had been greeted individually and lunch had been provided in the huge shop that had been cleared for this purpose, nothing would do but the boss must make a few public remarks. This he did with his customary ebullient delivery, and with the writer's apologies to an eighteenth century poet, if there were any who had come to scoff, they remained to pray, as he addressed them in the same language of the common man with which he had earlier talked to them. Had he been a politician, he would have got their votes; a football coach, his players would have triumphed; an evangelist, his congregation would have filled the offering plates. Instead, this billionaire summarized his own personal economic history and reminded his hearers of the old virtues of thrift, industry, and reward for doing hard work well for the benefit of self and country. It was an extraordinary manifestation of the creative and regenerative spirit of enterprise.

In September 1998, interviews and research for this project began. Just four months away from celebrating the completion of ninety full years, Jack Simplot was more than equal to the task of fielding questions about his past. Although there were subsequent changes in his physical condition, he appeared to be in excellent shape, standing just under six feet and weighing less than 200 pounds. In his top form, he later said, he stood about six feet and weighed about 210. Although he is bald on top now and keeps the sides clipped short giving the appearance of baldness, as a young man his full head of thick hair was dark brown, shading into black, and his eyes are still a sharp and penetrating blue. His physical presence was always impressive.

But there was always more to him than physical presence alone. Dr. W. W. Hall, Jr., who served as president of The College of Idaho (now Albertson College), came close to the mark when he wrote in *The Small College Talks Back* that he had just met a human dynamo named Jack Simplot.[3] Convinced that Simplot could help his college in significant ways, Hall secured him for its board of trustees, where he has served continuously since.

It is beyond the biographer's skill to isolate and define the source of this remarkable dynamism. Genetic? Perhaps, at least to an extent, for one can point to what geneticists call "hybrid vigor," that is, his calculating Yorkshire-English heritage in combination with the passion and imagination of his Gallic (French) blood line. If not nature, then nurture? One is inclined to respond “maybe,” knowing that this response, too, is not the whole answer. Certainly the time of his birth and the place where he grew up simply redounded with energy and optimism and the conviction that human endeavor could seize time by the forelock and make of it a servant.

But those are reductionist responses, to put the matter charitably, or simplistic, to use a current euphemism. The intellectual superiority (and moral too, as all would admit*) of the latter half of the twentieth century does not permit easy and stereotyped claims about national or linguistic or ethnic character. That sort of explanation might have been acceptable for Ralph Waldo Emerson, but we are so much smarter (and nicer) than our Victorian forebears that we would never perpetrate such a slander against human nature. Any attempt to account for this man's drive, zeal, and life-affirming energy by such a scheme as the foregoing will not work. Where does the element of luck come in? How should determination be factored into the trait of dynamism? Perhaps it is genetic; maybe it's a gift, unearned and unaccountable to anything but chance. Luck again. And judgment: is it related to dynamism? And if so, how? More than all this are elements like his wide-ranging intelligence and his ability to see farther than most of the rest of us.

How can one account for Jack Simplot's visionary ability to conceptualize, to dream beyond the scope of what is given most of us? The reader will not find the answers to these questions in this life story of one of

America's wealthiest men. What is offered instead is the material from which the reader may fashion a personal answer. That material has been selected—and biography as well as history, no matter how detailed, is selective—which reveals the man. That is to say that this work is not a history of the Simplot industries, even though there are few industrialists more closely identified with their industries than John Richard Simplot. In his own mind, he is what he has created, and what he has wrought is he.

The fact remains that there is something about this man that lingers in the imagination long after he has concluded the interview or given the talk or said his say. It is not doing violence to the Good Grey Poet to suggest that there is something intensely Whitmanian about Jack Simplot's love affair with the United States. He hears America singing; what he assumes, you shall assume; hold on to him and by God you shall not go down to defeat![4] The strong connection between free enterprise (*laissez faire*), of which Simplot is a vociferous advocate, and free verse (*vers libre*), for which Whitman is the international high priest, deserves more than a glancing comment. Dynamism and work and a democratic love of life throb and pulsate throughout both the art form and the economic system.

In the pages that follow, we shall see the European background of an American life, the translation of that life into a midwestern environment, and its transettlement into the American West. We shall note the development of irrigation and its importance to agriculture in that setting. Here, we shall see enterprise taking shape, deriving from and indebted to the most common of common vegetables yet one that is celebrated in both poetry and prose . . . the potato. And behind it all, running through it all, and holding everything together, we find the character and personality of John Richard Simplot.

Potato[5]

An underground grower, blind and common brown;
Got a misshapen look, it's nudged where it could;
Simple as soil yet crowded as earth with cell.
. . . .
Times being hard, the Sikh and the Senegalese,
Hobo and Okie, the body of Jesus the Jew,
Vestigial virtues, are eaten; we shall survive.

Three threads come together to create the texture of this biography and the fabric of the life of its subject. One cannot imagine Jack Simplot in a universe without potatoes. Potatoes require adequate water; by weight a potato is mostly water. The presence of water in the American West and a national policy in the first decade of the twentieth century that saw to its utility as a resource worthy of development through tax dollars were what brought the Simplot family from Iowa to Idaho, that and medical advice to flee tuberculosis. The third thread is the character trait of independence, but that is a jejeune way to put the matter.

Sociologist David Riesman identifies this trait as inner-directedness, and while a fuller discussion of it will be given at the appropriate place, we need to understand now that a youth absorbing from his elders a sense of worth and a respect for work will sometimes—often, perhaps—rebel against those very elders whose values he has internalized and light out on his own, just as Jack Simplot did at fourteen.

Potatoes, the Reclamation Act, inner-directedness: these are helpful in talking about J. R. Simplot.

In a strange but compelling way, *Growth of the Soil* by the Norwegian Nobel laureate Knut Hamsun is pertinent here. We can think of Simplot Soilbuilders, the great fertilizer part of the Simplot enterprise, and that is certainly a connection. The application of fertilizer is essential to the health of the soil, enriching marginal earth and replacing nutrients consumed by the growing of crops. But soil grows in and through the human life it sustains. Pioneers establish roots, literal and figurative, and through their labor a land and nation come into being. Another connection is that which resounds through Hamsun's celebration of the potato as a new staff of life. A brief quotation secures this point as Isak, a pioneer in Norway's near-wilderness, reflects upon this new food source he has planted:

"What was that about potatoes? Were they just a thing from foreign parts, like coffee; a luxury, an extra? Oh, the potato is a lordly fruit; a drought or downpour, it grows and grows all the same. It laughs at the weather, and will stand anything; only deal kindly with it, and it yields fifteen-fold again. Not the blood of a grape, but the flesh of a chestnut, to be boiled or roasted, used in every way. A man may lack corn [grain] to make bread, but give him potatoes and he will not starve."[6]

* * *

Preface Notes

*One must be cautious in using irony. The biographer does not really mean that the present age is smarter and nicer than the age that produced Ralph Waldo Emerson. It does indeed appear that the present age has more information at hand than did its ancestors (the information explosion) but is more vulnerable to moral posturing (political correctness) than were its forebears.

Two additional comments about language. Nowhere in this book will be found overtones of the linguistic legacy of the hippy decades. Take the word "opt," for example. Imagine its infinitive form : to opt. There are other and better choices—to choose, to decide, to elect, or, in its compound form ("to opt out") to withdraw. "Like" will be used as a preposition, not a conjunction. The traditional principal parts of such verbs as sink and kneel and weave and sneak (sink, sank, sunk; kneel, knelt, knelt; weave, wove, woven; sneak, sneaked, sneaked) will be used, if, indeed, they are called forth. If "doable" must be used, it will be hyphenated thus: "do-able," lest it be thought a strange hybrid describing one who is able to play the dobro.

Finally, in several places in the book Mr. Simplot speaks for himself. His language is so characteristic of the man that it is seldom edited. When suspension points appear, they usually indicate an editorial choice to condense, to supply a correct reading, or to indicate a hesitation in the flow of the monolog. His vocabulary is derived from Old English—direct, salty, replete with four-letter words, like the speech of military barracks or college campuses across the nation. In its less egregious examples it is reminiscent of the language of Walt Whitman, whom he never read, as these lines from the poet's Preface to the 1855 Edition of *Leaves of Grass* suggest: "The English language befriends the grand American expression . . . [suspension points in the original] it is brawny enough and limber enough and full enough. On the tough stock of a race who through all change of circumstances was never without the idea of political liberty, which is the animus of all liberty, it has attracted the terms of daintier and gayer and subtler and more elegant tongues. It is the powerful language of resistance . . . it is the dialect of common sense. It is the speech of the proud and melancholy races and of all who aspire. It is the chosen tongue to express growth faith [no commas in the original] self-esteem freedom justice equality friendliness amplitude prudence decision and courage. It is the medium that shall well nigh express the inexpressible."

1. It is likely that this really happened . . . more than once. In an interesting 1948 treatment of Jack Simplot, Richard L. Neuberger ("Idaho's Fantastic Millionaire," *Saturday Evening Post,* June 19) writes: "When he flew over a range [of grazing sheep] he ordered his pilot to come down . . . near the ranch house and he bought the outfit for $145,000," clearing that much the first two years he owned it. (110)

2. Quoted in George Gilder, *The Spirit of Enterprise* (New York: Simon and Schuster, 1984) 38.

3. (New York: Richard E. Smith, 1951) 166.

4. The reader might like to take a quick look at *Leaves of Grass* (1855), especially the part titled "Song of Myself," to gain a sharper understanding of this quality of dynamism.

5. These lines were written by Richard Wilbur, one of America's most significant poets of the middle years of the 20th century. Taking for his subject one of nature's humblest products, Wilbur subtly introduces ideas of nourishment, survival (even in war-torn and defeated lands), and something akin to salvation through this common vegetable. Artistically, the poem is built on accurate sense perceptions, suggesting that perhaps everything has a meaning which may be opened to us by observation. The entire text follows:

An underground grower, blind and common brown;
Got a misshapen look, it's nudged where it could;
Simple as soil yet crowded as earth with cell.

Cut open raw, it looses a cool clean stench,
Mineral acid seeping from pores of prest meal;
It is like breaching a strangely refreshing tomb:

Therein the taste of first stones, the hands of dead slaves,
Waters men drank in the earliest frightful woods,
Flint chips, and peat, and the cinders of buried camps.

Scrubbed under faucet water the planet skin
Polishes yellow, but tears to the plain insides;
Parching, the white's blue-hearted like hungry hands.

All of the cold dark kitchen, and war-frozen gray
Evening at window; I remember so many
Pealing potatoes quietly into chipt pails.

"It was potatoes saved us, they kept us alive."
Then they had something to say akin to praise
For the mean earth-apples, too common to cherish or steal.

Times being hard, the Sikh and the Senegalese,
Hobo and Okie, the body of Jesus the Jew,
Vestigial virtues, are eaten; we shall survive.

What has not lost its savor shall hold us up,
And we are praising what saves us, what fills the need.
(Soon there'll be packets again, with Algerian fruits.)

Oh, it will not bear polish, the ancient potato,
Needn't be nourished by Caesars, will blow anywhere,
Hidden by nature, counted-on, stubborn and blind.

You may have noted the bush that it pushes to air,
Comical-delicate, sometimes with second-rate flowers
Awkward and milky and beautiful only to hunger.

6. Translated from the Norwegian by W. W. Worster (New York: Random House, 1921) 45.

Simplot Family Tree

1 John Richard "Jack" SIMPLOT
B: 4 Jan 1909
P: Dubuque,Dubuque,IA
M: Dec 1930
P: Ontario,Malheur,OR
D:
P:

Ruby ROSEVEAR
(Spouse of no. 1)

2 Charles Richard SIMPLOT
B: 2 Jun 1883
P: Dubuque,Dubuque,IA
M: 4 Jan 1904
P: Dubuque,Dubuque,IA
D: Jun 1974
P:

3 Dorothy HAXBY
B: 31 Dec 1883
P: LaMotte,Jackson,IA
D: 3 Jun 1945
P: Caldwell,Canyon,ID

4 Charles LeClere SIMPLOT
B: 24 Apr 1838
P: Dubuque,Dubuque,IA
M: 1865
P: Dubuque,Dubuque,IA
D: 2 Dec 1900
P: Dubuque,Dubuque,IA

5 Mary Ellen BONSON
B: 1844/1845
P: Dubuque,Dubuque,IA
D: 6 Jan 1892
P: Dubuque,Dubuque,IA

6 Cornelius HAXBY
B: 10 Jan 1846
P: Dubuque,Dubuque,IA
M: 1870/1872
P: Iowa
D: 3 May 1915
P: LaMotte,Jackson,IA

7 Jane NELSON
B: 26 Nov 1848
P: Yorkshire,England
D: 3 Nov 1905
P: LaMotte,Jackson,IA

8 Henry SIMPLOT
B: 1 Mar 1806
P: Besancon,France
M: 17 May 1831
P: Parish,St. Lawrence,NY
D: 25 Dec 1846
P: Dubuque,Dubuque,IA

9 Susan LECLERE
B: 17 Mar 1811
P: Monte Belliard,France
D: 3 Apr 1876
P: Dubuque,Dubuque,IA

10 Richard BONSON
B: 1814
P: Reeth,Yorkshire,England
M: 1837/1838
P: Galena,Jo Daviess,IL
D: 1883
P: Dubuque,Dubuque,IA

11 Jane BURTON
B:
P: Bonsall,Derbyshire,England
D:
P: Dubuque,Dubuque,IA

12 John/William HAXBY
B:
P:
M:
P:
D:
P:

13 Dorothy BRADLEY
B:
P: Leeds,Yorkshire,England
D:
P: Cedar Bluffs,Saunders,NE

14 ? LUND
B:
P: England
M:
P:
D:
P:

15 Elizabeth NELSON
B: 10 Oct 1824
P: Yorkshire,England
D: 2 Feb 1895
P: LaMotte,Jackson,IA

Information provided by Margaret Simplot Clayville

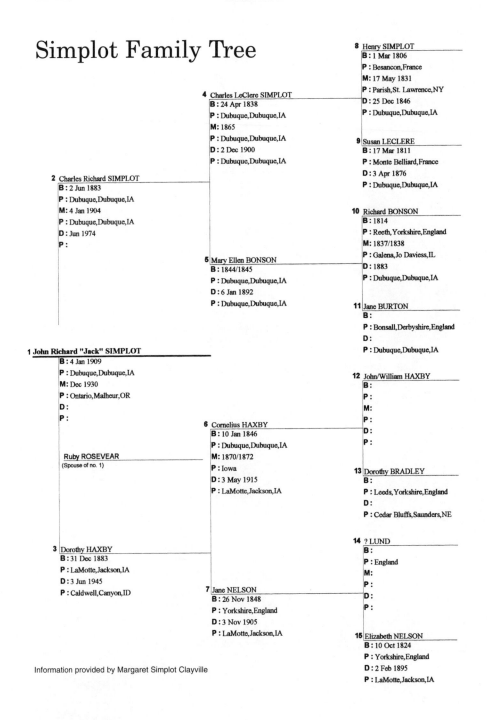

Chapter One

Antecedents

The story of Jack Simplot begins abroad, as do the stories of all Americans, there being no such thing as "native Americans," unless one counts primitive camels and other even older life forms. All homo sapients came from across the water, some recently, others by way of land bridges (or some would argue by boats) long ago. But we are all emigrants or their descendants. The Simplot family traces its origins to France and to England, two nations whose connections with each other have not always been cordial. As developed in a handwritten family history by Margaret Simplot Clayville, Jack's oldest sister, the story goes like this.[1]

Joseph Le Clere, a captain in the select cavalry of Napoleon, had been left for dead on a battlefield in Austria in two feet of snow and with twenty sword "and saber" wounds. When he saw a beggar walking among the wounded, clubbing them to death while collecting their watches, money, and jewelry, he must have thought his time had come. He was saved, however, by the intervention of three Austrian women searching among the wounded for those who might be saved. Joseph was chosen.

Taken to the home of an Austrian family, he regained something of his health, and here the daughter of the household fell in love with him. However, she was told by Joseph that he would return to France to marry his betrothed, Catherine Bourquin. He was sent to Paris, and for the remainder of his military career he was a home guardsman, a policeman. Although his health was never robust after this ordeal, he married Catherine, and they had a son named George F. Le Clere.

In the course of time George Le Clere grew up, married a girl named Catherine Belea, and while living in Dampierre the couple had a child March 17, 1811, a daughter whom they named Susan Le Clere. With her mother, Susan came to America about 1828 in the sheephold of a sailing vessel, settling in New York, where she met and married Henry Simplot. He was the great-grandfather of John Richard Simplot, the Jack who is the subject of this biography.

Henry Simplot—one would pronounce the name something like SamPLOH—was born March 1, 1806, in Besancón, a city in eastern France, not far from the Swiss border. (The c in this name attaches to a cedilla; the name is pronounced something like "Baysansonh.") When Henry was about sixteen, he sailed to America, settling for a time at Parish, New York, where he met and married Susan Le Clere on May 17, 1831. That he was Catholic and she

Protestant did not diminish the joy these two expatriates must have found in each other, and one can imagine their satisfaction in conversing in French, that "most meagre and inharmonious of all languages," according to Horace Walpole.[2]

After their sojourn in New York, the couple moved to Illinois to a spot on the Chicago River near Lake Michigan, where they built a log cabin. After a year or two, they sold the cabin for $200 and moved to Nauvoo, Illinois. Their plans to move to Texas were altered when the steamboat on which they were passengers sailed up the river, not down, and they landed in Dubuque, Iowa, in 1836. The next year, 1837, their son, Alexander Simplot, was born earning the distinction of being "the first white boy born in Iowa," the kind of distinction local historians are eager to affirm. (Such claims are difficult to prove, and a special edition of the State Historical Society of Iowa publication *The Palimpsest* which discusses Simplot's work as a Civil War artist for *Harper's Weekly* makes no mention of "first white boy" status.[3])

Henry became a trader, a well-respected businessman, and one of Dubuque's first aldermen.[4] He died suddenly on Christmas Day 1846. When Susan Le Clere Simplot sold her interests following his death, writes Margaret Simplot Clayville, the author of this family history, she put the money in silver and gold coin under the bed in a bushel basket.

Alexander Simplot, Jack's great uncle, attended school in Dubuque, Iowa and Rock River Seminary, matriculated at Union College, Schenectady, New York, and graduated from it in 1858. Always interested in art, he nevertheless began a career as a teacher in Dubuque, a career that was interrupted for about two years (1861-1863) while he served as Special Artist for *Harper's Weekly*, having more than fifty Civil War sketches published before illness forced him to abandon this important work.[5] He was a gifted artist, and his Civil War scenes are among the finest ever done.

Charles Le Clere Simplot, Alexander's younger brother and Jack's grandfather, was born April 24, 1838, in Dubuque. As a young man, he was engaged in mining. He served from 1861-1863 in the Iowa State Militia, joining the 46th Iowa Volunteers on May 2, 1864, in which he served as commissary sergeant and acting quartermaster. He was discharged honorably September 23, 1864, having met the terms of his enlistment—"100 days or the duration." In April of 1867, Charles married Mary Ellen Bonson (born Dubuque, c. 1844), daughter of Richard Bonson, one of Dubuque's oldest and most honored settlers. They had five children—Susan, Henry, Jane, Charles Richard, and Benjamin—all of whom died in their youth, excepting only Charles Richard Simplot, Jack's father.

It is here that the English connection is established. Richard Bonson was born at Reeth (Margaret renders this as "Reetle") near Richmond in Swaledale, Yorkshire, which was a nineteenth century lead-mining center. Richard, the son of Robert Bonson, emigrated to America in 1832 when he was eighteen, in the company of miners and their wives heading for Galena, Illinois, in search of lead deposits. At home in Swaledale, lead mining became seriously depressed around 1830 and by 1865 it was finished, causing large-scale emigration.[6] When Richard saw the primitive way lead was smelted in Galena, he went back to England to study carefully the modern English techniques. When he returned to Illinois, he was accompanied by his parents and four of his older sisters and their husbands. His mother, Mary Spensley Bonson, died of cholera while traveling up the Mississippi River and was buried on an island across from St. Louis in a grave which could never be relocated.

The sisters and families stayed at Galena, but Richard went on to Dubuque, Iowa, batching in a log cabin at Rockdale, where he, his father, and several other men built a lead-smelting furnace. In fact, as Margaret tells us, in 1836 they built three furnaces. The industry must have been booming, for there proved to be many complications in locating claims and establishing ownership. To resolve these problems, a committee of twenty-five men was appointed to arbitrate and settle these difficulties. An executive committee of three was selected from the larger committee, and Richard was one of them.

In May of 1837 or 1838 Richard married Jane Burton at Galena, Illinois, and the couple returned to Dubuque by horseback to a log cabin, primitive by any standard. It had, for instance, windows with shutters but no glass panes. Here they lived on corn meal and prairie chickens while they put every dollar they could back into their business. Richard continued to build furnaces in Iowa and Illinois, investing as he was able in government land at a dollar an acre. When Iowa gained statehood in 1846, Richard became a state senator. As prosperity came, he built a house of brick (some of his shot towers were also constructed of brick) shipped up the Mississippi from St. Louis. This residence on his farm near Asbury Road was about six miles from Dubuque, and here he lived with Jane and daughters Priscilla and Mary Ellen. In addition to his activity in lead smelting, an enterprise that claimed his interest for forty-five years, Bonson helped with the first Iowa railroad, assisted in the establishment of banks, and gained considerable respect as a merchant.

In 1866 Jane Burton Bonson died, and two years later Richard married Mrs. Harriet Watts Pearson, a wealthy widow from Manchester, England, who was visiting a cousin. Upon returning from their European honeymoon, Richard built a mansion, the "elegant" and "attractive" Burnege Villa. As his real estate and banking interests claimed more and more of his time, he gave up his duties in the state legislature. Three children were born to this union, Robert, William, and Anna. After much suffering from rheumatism, Richard died on February 1, 1883, following kidney stone surgery.

Bonson had a sterling reputation, writes Margaret Clayville, hating lies and dishonesty. This family historian says that his motto was "Do right," and, affronted once by a man who was trying to cheat him over a dollar, knocked the man down.

Mary Ellen Bonson was born in either Dubuque or its near neighbor Rockdale, in or about 1844. As befit the daughter of prosperous parents, she was given the best education available, graduating from the fashionable ladies' finishing school in Epworth, Iowa, and traveling abroad.

On March 26, 1867, she married Charles Le Clere Simplot, "quite a French dandy in his time," according to the family historian. Their happy life was clouded by Charles's speculations in his brother Alexander's grain-buying activities in which Charles lost his home and all his inheritance. When Richard Bonson learned of the misfortune, he bought the house and farm from whoever took it and deeded it to Mary Ellen and her heirs with instructions she was never to sign another paper without consulting her father. This directive caused a rift between her father, Richard Bonson, and her husband, Charles, who refused to allow Mary Ellen ever again to go see her father. Because Mary and her father had been very close, this separation was a great sorrow to them both.

The children of Mary Ellen Bonson Simplot and Charles Le Clere Simplot were stalked by the white plague. Jane Burton Simplot died when she was sixteen, Fred died a year later, and the next year twenty-one-year-old Susan died. Thus did consumption, the phthisic, hectic fever—TB went by many names—ravage this generation of Simplots.

Charles Richard Simplot, Jack's father, said that about the only thing he remembered concerning his mother was how worried she was when his little brother Benjamin was ill, and the death of this baby left her understandably depressed. She caught a severe cold and died on January 6, 1892. It was then that Charles Richard "Dick" Simplot, Mary's nine-year-old son, was placed under the care of a Scotswoman, a widow named Mrs. Richards, his own health despaired of.

However, Dick Simplot did not succumb; instead, he hunted and fished along Catfish Creek and the Mississippi River, learning the ways and haunts of small game and riverine life and living a pleasant Tom Sawyer-like existence. The shot towers were a diversion for him, and he played in them. School ended for him when he was in the sixth grade. When he was sixteen, his foster mother took him to Scotland, a remarkable experience for a kid from Iowa. It was an extensive trip, with young Simplot visiting many places associated with Scottish history and trying to adjust his ear to a dialect so very different from that which was his Iowa birthright.

By this time, Mrs. Richards had re-married, and Dick did not care for Mr. Hoskins. Mr. Hoskins was more than hostile to young Simplot, threatening on one occasion to kill him. (In 1933 when Rob Bonson, an uncle from Dubuque visited the Simplots in Idaho, he laughingly observed that Dick could now return to Dubuque since "Old Hoskins is dead.")

Upon returning to Dubuque, Dick began doing farm work for a family named Miller. To assist the family at the birth of one of their many children, a Mrs. Haxby's services were engaged, and this woman's friendly manner and helpful efficiency impressed Dick. In the course of time at church and later at parties, he met the rest of her family, of whom Dorothy, about his own age, held a special attraction for him.

When his uncles Will and Rob Bonson offered him a job with Iowa Iron Works, Dick accepted it and was forced to rent a horse and buggy or a team and cutter from the town livery stable to drive out to court Dorothy. The horses indeed knew the way to carry the sleigh, and young Simplot, who sometimes fell asleep driving back to town after seeing Dorothy home, would be delivered by the team to the livery stable door. In the winter if it were necessary to combat the cold, he would knot the lines behind his head and run behind the cutter, riding on the back when it was necessary to catch his breath.

Finally, on January 4, 1904, the young couple tied another kind of knot, and at this point we must look at the background of the girl who would become the mother of one of America's wealthiest men. Interestingly enough, another Yorkshire connection appears. Jack Simplot had "Tyke" (the folk name for people from Yorkshire) ancestors on both his maternal and paternal lines of descent. Both his father's mother and his mother's mother derived from that English county, as did his mother's grandmother (Jack's great-grandmother).

The popular television series *All Creatures Great and Small*, dealing with the veterinary practice of Dr. James Herriot and associates, has given Yorkshire a currency it has not always enjoyed. One of England's northernmost counties and its largest, Yorkshire has an undeserved reputation—this is also true of its near-neighbor Scotland (only two counties separate them)—for stinginess. An official at the University of Leeds once jokingly observed that a Yorkshireman was a Scot with all the generosity squeezed out of him, and a popular bit of Yorkshire folk wisdom declares, "If tha's ever bound to do owt, never do owt for nowt, but do it for thysen."[7] That is, if you are ever going to do something, never do it for nothing, but do it for yourself. A Yankee might have said, "Mind the main chance." Jack Simplot's record of philanthropy is a story in itself.

Dorothy Ann Haxby was the product of the union of Jane Nelson, born November 1, 1848, in Yorkshire, England, and Cornelius Haxby, born in Dubuque County, Iowa, 1846. Cornelius was the son of a John (his name might have been William) Haxby and Dorothy Bradley Haxby, born in Leeds, England. Jane was the daughter of a divorced parent, Elizabeth Nelson, and a man identified by Margaret Simplot Clayville only as "Lund," either his surname or given name. A strong Swedish or at least Scandinavian background is suggested, either way: " __?___ Lund" or "Lund Nelson." Whatever his real name, Lund proved not to be the kind of man Elizabeth had thought he was, so she divorced him and moved to the United States where she lived with her brother and reared her daughter Jane.

This American blend—Dick and Dorothy Simplot—moved to their farm where they began the life of hard work farmers have always experienced. In the horse-powered economy of 1904, any activity that might produce income was grist for the farmer's mill—grain crops, hogs, chickens, turkeys, ducks, geese, hay for the domestic animals and as a cash crop. They milked eighteen cows, and Dick hauled the milk to Dubuque, sharing this chore with his neighbors so that Dick's turn came up every six days. On this day, the couple would get up at 4 a.m. To finance the operation, Dick, backed by an old Civil War buddy of his father's, secured a loan, borrowing money at six percent. Margaret quotes her father: "My credit has been good ever since. That has been our greatest success. We always paid our debts. We were always good for the money we borrowed."

Children came along. Margaret Jane, "Peggy," Simplot was born June 29, 1906. Myrtle Simplot was born August 14, 1907.

It is difficult for a modern reader fully to comprehend the difficulties facing a young mother of two toddlers, a helper who was expected to cook, garden, can and otherwise preserve the produce, besides help with the haying and the milking. Aside from the viciously hard labor, a cloud hung over this young family. It is likely that as his family grew and his responsibilities increased, Dick's thoughts turned with increasing frequency to the untimely deaths by tuberculosis of his siblings. When a physician suggested that a move to a drier climate might be the way to escape the white plague, a new dynamic was introduced into this young man's consciousnes. West of the 100th meridian . . . that way lay safety.

Chapter One Notes

1. The Simplot family history is contained in various thick ledgers, written in ink at different times, and not all contain the same information. The biographer relied heavily upon the heavy volume in Jack Simplot's possession which he considers the "ur-text." Consisting of intermingled un-numbered pages of text, genealogy and photographs, the volume challenges conventional documentation. The biographer acknowledges his debt to the family historian with deep appreciation. Incidentally, Charles Richard Simplot's birth on June 2, 1883, was just one year before the American publication of *The Adventures of Huckleberry Finn.*

2. Quoted in Robert McCrum, William Cran, and Robert MacNeil, *The Story of English* (New York: Penguin Books 1986) 44.

3. January 1965.

4. Richard Martin, "Alexander Simplot—Artist," *The Palimpsest*, 7.

5. "Alexander Simplot—Artist," 9.

6. *James Herriot's Yorkshire* (New York: St. Martin's Press, 1979) 100.

7. The proverb was collected in Leeds, England, by the biographer from Rowland Parkin, custodian of the Headingly Methodist Church—denominated a chapel by those who recognize only one church, the Church of England, although grudging recognition is accorded the Roman Catholic and the Orthodox churches—while Bruern Fellow at the University of Leeds 1971-72.

Chapter Two

The Westward Migration

Tuberculosis has been around a very long time. In Selman A. Waksman's authoritative *The Conquest of Tuberculosis*, the author titles his first chapter "Since Time Immemorial Man Has Been Afflicted by a Dreadful Disease, Variously know as Phthisis, Scrofula, Consumption, and Tuberculosis," a rather lengthy but so very accurate summation of the historical connection between homo sapiens and this disease.[1]

Tuberculosis was common in ancient Greece and Rome and as recently as 1655 it accounted for more than one-fifth of all deaths in London.[2] It was not until 1865 that a French scientist named Jean-Antone Villemin demonstrated it to be caused not by a malevolent nocturnal influence (*la influenza*) or heredity (or any one of a number of imagined causes) but by a specific germ.[3] Even so, the villain Mycobacterium tuberculosis was not isolated and identified until 1882, when Robert Koch, a German, presented his proof at a meeting of the Physiological Society of Berlin on

March 4.[4] This was just one year before Charles Richard Simplot was born.

But even though the organism was identified, its defeat lay far in the future. A reasonable strategy for controlling it was the sanatorium treatment whose patron saint was Dr. Edward L. Trudeau, and for many years, from about 1885 to about 1943, his establishment at Saranac Lake, New York, served as the model for this mode of treating the disease, particularly in its pulmonary form.[5] Within twenty-five years of the founding at Saranac, there were over 400 such retreats.[6] While it is not necessary to describe in detail the regimen of Trudeau's treatment, one aspect of it is significant because it is laden with ironic implications.

Not problematic at all were such things as rest, fresh air, the out-of-doors, and a wholesome diet, including plenty of milk. Actually, milk had been recommended to TB sufferers for centuries, especially woman's milk and if that were not available then warm cow's or ass's or goat's milk.[7] Waksman says that John Wesley in his *Primitive Physick* recommended "that the patient 'in the last stages [of treatment] suck an healthy woman daily,' a procedure that had cured his father, he said."[8] But an irony lies in the fact that milk is one of the most common sources of TB infection.

A factsheet by Dr. Mitchel Essey, of the U.S. Department of Agriculture, encapsulates pertinent information to the effect that TB is caused by three types of bacteria and that of these the bovine—

M. bovis—can affect all vertebrates. It exists significantly in unpasteurized milk from infected cows.[9]

In 1917 a cooperative program of state-federal TB eradication was begun, and that program with its emphasis on the testing of cattle together with improved sanitation, the discovery of effective drugs, and pasteurization of milk, has greatly reduced the incidence of TB.[10] In 1917, Jack Simplot was eight years old. Dick and Dorothy and their young family were fortunate to have escaped the disease that had claimed Dick's siblings. The word "escaped" is the appropriate word, for none of the foregoing scientific information had been discovered yet; they believed their only real hope of escaping the disease lay in their move to a dry climate.

It was a common belief, advanced and sustained by medical opinion. Western literature and the life it reflects are replete with pulmonary sufferers who made the move west for the sake of their health. Waksman cites a writer named Long on this point: "Many of the most progressive pushing and wealthy business men of Southern Arizona left their north-eastern homes and came here as confirmed invalids, with the hope of dying easily. They would not die now for ten times what they are worth."[11] Harold Bell Wright and Zane Grey did not invent the "lunger"; they discovered him.

But where in the healthful Western climate, the home of deer and antelope, mustangs and range cattle, could a young farmer hope to make a living? The answer to that question requires a somewhat detailed look at another cultural phenomenon of the first decade of the twentieth century: the Reclamation Act and the growth of irrigation and agriculture west of the 100th meridian. East of that imaginary marker, farmers relied upon nature—precipitation at the right time—to provide the moisture required for crops to grow.

The story begins earlier, with the Homestead Act of 1862, signed by our martyred sixteenth president. This act allotted an apparently generous 160 acres per claim, a generous amount if one were accustomed to farm production east of the 100th meridian. However, along the 100th meridian is an observable borderline west of which annual precipitation begins to be less than twenty inches per year. That amount required changes in farming strategy, and even the rediscovery of dry farming techniques could not provide the farmer who had moved west from Iowa or Illinois adequate bushels per acre. Clearly, more acres were essential in order to wrest a livelihood from the dry soil.

Fifteen years later in 1877 the Desert Land Act, directed to the thirteen western states, increased the allotment to 320 acres per claimant to be developed through irrigation. One may wonder why it took so long for lawmakers to realize that the West was different in several respects from the other regions of the United States, and one of these was that it was much drier. But it is only fair to point out here that for a number of years the official policy of the government with respect to agriculture and its practices was based squarely on superstition. That superstition is encapsulated in the proverb "Rain follows the plow." It was believed, it came to be the official government policy, that the practice of agriculture would alter weather patterns and that where the plow was put into the soil, heaven would reward the efforts with its blessing in the form of rain. Charles Dana Wilber wrote in 1881 a book titled *The Great Valleys and Prairies of Nebraska and the Northwest* in which he said the following:

"Not by any magic or enchantment, not by incantations or offerings, but, instead, in the sweat of his face, toiling with his hands, man can persuade the heavens to yield their treasure of dew and rain upon the land he has chosen for his dwelling place.

"It is indeed a grand consent, or, rather, concert of forces—the human energy or toil, the vital seed, and the polished raindrop that never fails to fall to the imploring power or prayer of labor."[12]

All of this was anticipating an agricultural West, a West of the future when crops would be planted in a fertile and productive soil and their harvest would assure the farmer of a livelihood. What predominated instead was an altogether different pattern, a transhumant livestock West. Briefly, the pattern worked like this:

Permanent EuroAmerican settlement in the interior American West, excepting that of the Mormons, is generally observed to have been a backwash phenomenon of frustrated westward emigrants to the Willamette Valley, dejected California gold-rushers, and various others who, upon reaching the western limits of the continent, were disappointed in what was left to them. So they headed east, back across the lands over which they had initially hurried west as fast as they could travel to get to the promised land of Oregon. Back in the interior west, those who did not try mining generally had two opportunities. They could adapt to the environment by becoming ranchers in the California mode—herds of cattle or horses and later, sheep, with a central ranch house and unlimited access to free public range. Or they could become small-scale farmers by developing local shoestring patterns of irrigation. By means of diversion dams or waterwheels and gravity, water was taken out upstream and used to irrigate as much of the valley downstream as possible. This sort of irrigation pattern assumed a shoestring appearance, long and narrow, irregular, and practically limited to the flood plain of the stream. Later, dams were constructed for two reasons: to help guarantee water after spring runoff and to provide a source of water for areas above the riparian.[13]

By the use of this kind of irrigation, early settlers had remarkable though small-scale success with orchards and with such traditional crops as hay and grain. Hay was usually reserved for winter feed for saddle and draft horses and for milk cows. Range animals got along quite well subsisting on native bunch grasses through the winter, barring the occurrence of killer winters like those of 1886-87 in the Great Plains and 1889-90 in the Intermountain Northwest.

And generally throughout the dry American West, the pattern, or some variation of it, worked. But the scale was generally small, and arid western agricultural land was not being settled, even with the Homestead and Desert Entry acts. Then in 1894 Congress passed the Carey Act through which the federal government ceded as much as one million acres to any western state that would assume the responsibility for reclaiming, that is, irrigating, those acres.[14] Southern Idaho seemed the proper place to test the provisions of the Carey Act, and within a few years the Snake River was dammed (Milner Dam) and the Twin Falls Land and Water Company contracted with the state to develop 270,000 acres, private capital, of course, coming from the east.[15]

The next important development in the reclamation of the American West, of which the developments in the Snake River Basin were characteristic, was the enactment of what is popularly known as the National Reclamation Act in 1902. Now the energies of the nation were focused upon getting water to the desert; irrigation became a national priority. The Snake River's Minidoka Project, whose canal and system of distribution were completed in 1907, supplied the first irrigation water made available by the U.S. Reclamation Service and was the first of a long series of joint ventures combining federal, state, local, and private interests.[16] In Idaho a total of 4,000,000 acres have been affected by the actions of the federal government (1,500,000 acres by projects of the Bureau of Reclamation, 600,000 by the Carey Act, 1,900,000 by the Desert Land Act), in Washington 1,600,000 acres have been affected, and in Oregon the figure is 1,900,000. [17]

Word of this new farm land in the West reached into America's heartland, and shortly an Iowa family would utilize the railroad's emigrant train and move to a country where the air was dry and salubrious and where farming, irrigated farming, could be practiced. The Simplots would go west, along with many other Iowans.

Indeed, they were both preceded and followed in their migration by many Iowans. One family name springs immediately to mind in this connection, that of Idaho's former governor Frank Steunenberg, who had been murdered some five years before the Simplot transettlement. He was but one of a large family to have settled in Caldwell, Idaho.

In his detailed social history of the first decade of the twentieth century, J. Anthony Lucas mentions that dinner guests at the A. K. Steunenberg home on Christmas Day 1905 included no fewer than thirty with that name, all claiming an Iowa connection.[18] In an article titled "Irrigation Agriculture in Idaho as Seen by Hanry A. Wallace in 1909," by Richard Lowitt, young Wallace, future Secretary of Agriculture, is presented as undertaking an assignment for his father's farm journal to examine irrigation agriculture and describe how Midwesterners were succeeding with this new thing. He visited the Payette-Boise Project and also the Minidoka and Twin Falls projects, finding Iowa farmers willing to share their experience with him. [19]

But prudence dictated caution for this Iowa family. In the summer of 1907, therefore, Dick Simplot and John Haxby, a brother-in-law, took the train to Washington to visit Robert Haxby, who had moved to Sunnyside in that state. On this trip they visited Seattle with its plank streets and fir forests, saw the lordly Columbia River where at Celilo Falls native fishermen took life-sustaining salmon, and were more than a bit disappointed in Mountain Home, Idaho. They returned home to reflect upon what they had seen, and in the winter of 1909 on January 4, Dick and Dorothy's third child, first boy, was born. He was named John Richard, and he would be the last of their children to be born in Iowa.

In February the family made its decision to move west, and Dick sent his hired man with two emigrant cars of livestock and farm machinery to Washington. Here farms were productive, but prices for farm goods were depressed. That summer, Dick and his father-in-law, Cornelius Haxby, went to Oregon to look over prospects there, and although there were timber claims which could be filed upon, lumber companies were involved, requiring potential settlers to sign up with them. The result was that Dick took a desert entry claim of 300 acres near either Bend or Madras, which he ultimately abandoned.

Early in the spring of 1910, Dick went to Burley, Idaho, where he bought a lot on Overland and 18th streets, building a shed to live in during the summer while he worked on a proper house. Dorothy and the three children came from Iowa later in the spring with Robert Haxby and his family.

For the next months Dick farmed south of Burley while building three more houses there, one of which he traded to Dave Bennnett for the "home place" at Springdale. Bennett had put in years holding the place and clearing nearly twenty acres of the eighty-acre farm. He had only a few months left in which to prove up on his claim, but he could not do so, for he was in jail accused of horse-stealing.

Dick Simplot was a hard-working man, farming, leveling land for irrigation, removing sagebrush, and building houses. This ambition helped establish his reputation in the community, a reputation that was helped along by two circumstances. In the first place, he had money enough from the sale of his Iowa farm (Jack estimates six or seven thousand dollars) to prove that he was a solid member of the community, not a man who just got by. His reputation was likely furthered, moreover, by the $20,000 (worth fourteen or fifteen times that amount in current dollars or more than $300,000) which Cornelius had settled upon Dorothy.[20] With Dick's encouragement Dorothy had put the money in postal savings in her own name (Dick lacked confidence in conventional banks). Although Dick never touched this money, the fact that it was there more than likely strengthened his reputation.

From their nice home on Overland, the family moved to a one-room log cabin with a dirt roof on Marsh Creek, the home place. Here Dick built on a lean-to with a tarpaper roof, and the family lived in those two rooms that first year. Like others who were building the land into productive farms, they burned sagebrush for both the cookstove and the space heater. They were not poor; this was simply the way to get ahead in that time and place.

It is difficult, perhaps impossible, to recover the quality of life as it was lived by our forebears. Attempts to provide "thick" descriptions of life then are likely to cause the eyelids of readers to fall shut as the contemporary audience comes to expect the old trite language of long ago, of how long a walk it was to the district school, which was uphill both ways with snow up to the tops of fence posts, and so on.

One way of evoking the quality of life of that time is to ask today's audience to visualize a southern Idaho landscape nearly barren of trees. After all, this land had only recently been range land, over which cattle, horses, and, later, sheep, roamed, and arboreal areas were limited to sprinklings of trees and bushes along springs and watercourses. It was sufficiently primitive that the Oregon Trail extended across the southeast corner of the place, and Dick could observe emigrant wagons still using it as a few prairie schooners swayed and jolted their way to Oregon. After the trees disappear from the mind's mental picture, the lawns and many of the fences should be erased. Instead of proper houses of bungalow or ranch or "I" style, most of the few dwellings were shacks and cabins surrounded by dirt with sticks stuck here and there which would become trees eventually.

Inside, perhaps the most notable feature in summer for more than a few homes was the presence of hordes of houseflies, so thick that one of the ways of removing them from the household was to open a door—of which there might be two or perhaps only one for the whole structure—while the children drove the creatures toward the opening by waving empty flour sacks or large pieces of cloth behind the retreating insects.

Instead of proper roads at just about every section line, trails snaked here and there, disappearing into the ubiquitous sagebrush. As to today's prominent power transmission poles and lines and telephone poles, most would be wiped from the cultural horizon of the first decade of this century. The country was very much like this in 1910, when Halley's Comet appeared and America's greatest writer, Mark Twain, died.

Jack Simplot was then, in the language of that stock-raising community, a long yearling.[21]

Chapter Two Notes

1. Berkeley and Los Angeles: University of California Press, 1964.

2. Waksman, 18-19.

3. Waksman, 82-83. 27

4. Waksman, 86.

5. Waksman, 94-95.

6. Waksman, 95.

7. Waksman, 56-57.

8. 57.

9. "Bovine Tuberculosis," U. S. Department of Agriculture, October 1995) 1-3.

10. "Bovine Tuberculosis," 2.

11. Waksman, 58.

12. Louie W. Attebery, "From Littoral to Lateral," *Idaho Yesterdays* (Spring-Summer, Vol. 30, No. 1-2, 1986) 26. Several of the following references derive from a special issue of *Idaho Yesterdays*, the quarterly journal of the Idaho State Historical Society, an issue that derived from papers read at a conference on "Irrigation in Idaho" that was sponsored by the Snake River Regional Studies Center of what is now Albertson College of Idaho. The conference was held in Boise on March 26 and 27, 1986. Cooperating entities included Albertson College of Idaho through its Regional Studies Center, the Idaho Water Resource Board, and the Idaho Humanities Council.

13. 28-29.

14. Leonard Arrington, "Irrigation in the Snake River Valley: An Historical Overview," *IY*, 4-5.

15. 6.

16. 6.

17. John Rosholt, "Irrigation and Politics," *IY*, 21.

18. *Big Trouble* (New York: Simon & Schuster, 1997) 48.

19. (*IY* 35, 1 Spring 1991) 23.

20. JRS, 9-24-98, tape 3, side A. Albertson College of Idaho Emeritus Professor of Economics W. LaMar Bollinger points out the difficulties of expressing the value of one age's currency in terms of another's. He notes the importance of the qualifying word "approximately." In 1910, $20,000 was truly a substantial amount of money.

21. Readers should not be surprised to learn that the Oregon Trail continued to be used well into the twentieth century. Margaret Clayville writes that her father recalled seeing Ezra Meeker in Burley in 1912, traveling from Portland, Oregon, to Washington, D. C. marking the route for the Lincoln Highway, U.S. 30, the paved version of the Oregon Trail. Meeker was using "Pathfinder," a White 12-cylinder automobile.

Chapter Three

Roots

Those were glorious days that first year, writes Margaret Clayville. In spite of the similarity of the names "Idaho" and "Iowa," close enough in spelling to cause much confusion, the two states are quite dissimilar. The Simplots must have noticed the dryness of the air, making manual labor in Idaho much easier to endure. Here, though the thermometer could reach triple digits, perspiration evaporated quickly. Back in Iowa, the humid heat clung to the body day and night; to perspire did not mean that one could gain relief. And although Idaho did not have fireflies to add magic to summer nights, it did offer cool temperatures as soon as the sun set, making sleep easy and restful.

Unlike Iowa, Idaho is mostly mountain terrain. The family hunted and fished, for game was plentiful. Sagehens and cottontail rabbits abounded, and in the late fall and winter ducks rose and clouded the sky at the sound of a shot or even at the clapping of hands. But there was always work. Clearing the land of the eternal sage was a first order of business, and this slow operation was undertaken by the use of a section of steel railroad rail drawn by a four-horse team. The sage that was broken off or pulled out was piled by hand, the roots grubbed out with a grubbing hoe, added to the piles, and what was not needed for cooking or for warmth was burned. After the land was cleared, it had to be leveled to make irrigation possible. Ditches were added, and water came in the next year, 1911.

Crops were good but did not produce much income, for there was no market. Along about 1913, the farmers got together and formed an organization called the Farmers' Society of Equity, an early attempt at getting farmers fair prices for their crops. Dick Simplot was a director of the organization for a time, later selling his stock to Jack.

But for now, it was a fairly steady diet of hard work. It is unfortunate that the family historian recorded so little of the sort of family folklore that helped create an identity for households of an earlier time. A reader would like to know what were the first words spoken by this round-cheeked little boy, what nursery rhymes he learned to recite, what mischief created by him made its way into family stories. We do know that his mother was a Presbyterian (the college that Jack has served more than fifty years was founded by Presbyterians), that she took her children to Sunday school, church, and the various activities in which families participated, this in view of the almost universal presence of the Mormon establishment.

Dorothy was musically talented, playing both the violin and piano. We know further that Jack was introduced to animals early, draft horses, saddle stock, milk cows, sheep, hogs, chickens. . . all of which required a good deal of work, and nearly all of which figure in the life story of this interesting man.

Though not plentiful, there is a residue of family lore in which young Jack figures prominently. In *Declo—My Town, My People*, compiled by the Declo History Committee, we read that Jack's father frequently had to bring the little boy into the house with the admonition to keep him inside because his curiosity made it impossible for Dick to conclude the repairs on machinery. Jack needed to see what his father was doing.[1]

Then there is the account of the Simplots buying their first automobile some time around 1915. The seller's efforts to explain to Dorothy the operation of the seven-passenger Studebaker equipped with jump seats were frustrated by Jack's crawling around, between, and among the seats because he needed to know what was going on.[2] Jack remembers an early experience with doctors and medicine:

> *We never went to doctors—never went to a doctor. Hell, we never thought about goin' to a doctor! No, no, I never was in a doctor's office till I cut that finger off. I got it in a pulley, and they loaded me in the wagon. I can remember like it was yesterday. I don't know how old I was, maybe two, three, four, somewhere in there, and it took us eight hours to get to town.*

> *It was dark, and I can remember going up the stairs. I remember the old doctor said, "Why didn't you bring the piece in? I coulda put it back on." And they said, "We looked for it, but the chickens had eaten it.*[3]

The injured finger was on the right hand. The first joint of the third finger is missing.

He was a bit older than this when he learned about buying goods on time. It may have been on his way to or from school, a two and one-fourth mile walk each way, that he saw and fell in love with a pair of rubber boots in the window of a local dry goods store. Black with a red trim around the top, those boots were just the ticket for keeping young feet dry. After days of admiring them from afar, the first-grader entered the store and bought the boots on time. The proprietor sent them home with the bill, and later that night Jack learned a serious lesson at his father's knee about the hazards of buying goods on credit, a lesson not unlike that of Ben Franklin's, who once paid too much for a whistle.[4]

He grew up doing the work most farm boys learned to do as children and adolescents. No writer has treated the subject of small boys doing a man's work in an earlier time better than Hamlin Garland. If the reader wants to be reminded of what it was like to be a boy yet expected to do a man's work, turn to "Under the Lion's Paw." It was not that the father wished to mistreat his son; there was no alternative. It did not occur to either the fictional father or son that such work might one day be construed as child abuse.

So Jack learned to drive a team and manage farm implements, harnessing and unharnessing his own horses, to accomplish which some farm youngsters had to stand on a wooden box, for they were too short to throw the harness onto a tall Percheron horse. They might, however, manage without the box to get the harness onto a shorter, blockier Belgian. Jack stood on a stool rather than on a wooden box.

With Dandy and Doll, a team Dick had brought from Iowa, Jack learned to mow, buckrake, and stack hay with an overshot stacker. He milked cows and fed calves with a bucket. He slopped hogs and assisted with the castration of them and young bull calves. He helped brand horses and cattle, and he helped perform other animal surgery, such as de-horning, a bloody job.

During harvest, he drove a binder or a header, depending upon which technology was then dominant. The former was a machine that cut and tied grain into bundles, the latter cut grain and deposited it into "boxes," wagons with one low side that were driven under a spout up which the headed grain was elevated into the wagon. He pitched bundles or drove a bundle wagon, pitching his load into the "turkey" of the separator, that is, the feeder or conveyor belt into the threshing machine. He learned the demanding job of sewing sacks of wheat neatly and quickly. He pumped water for the livestock, and he turned the handle of the cream separator; he might, if the occasion demanded, wash and scald the cream separator.

He fixed fence, and he rode after the cattle. During summer, there was always irrigating to tend to, and ditches needed to be cleaned and repaired. He ran a trap line, catching muskrats and preparing their skins. Thinning sugarbeets in the spring and topping them in the fall were ways of adding to a small hoard of money, that and digging, picking, and sorting potatoes. He could not have been lazy even if he had been so inclined. His father was a tough taskmaster, but Jack was equal to the tasks at hand. He may not have realized it at the time, but he was preparing for his independence.

Jack's only brother, Robert LeRoy Simplot, was born July 30, 1914, in Burley.

When asked about the cultural amenities of life around Declo, Idaho, in the teens of this century, Jack recalled:

> *We had a radio,. . . but my uncle had one of* [those] *phonographs with a big horn and the round discs. I couldn't have been more than three or four years old.* [in response to a question about country dances] *Oh, there* [were] *fiddlers and a lot of barn dancing. My old dad . . . we had one of the big barns . . . but he didn't believe in dancing. He thought the Mormons dancing in their church [were wrong]. Of course he was an atheist if there ever was one, and I don't think he was ever in a church. He was a Mason*[5] *and he'd take Mother and us three kids and drive us up to this little Sunday school they had in Declo, a one-room Sunday school . . . . In the winter we didn't go but in the summer we went pretty regular.*[6]

In the fall of 1917, the rhythms of farm life abruptly changed when Dick and Dorothy sold their farm to John Braden and moved to California.[7] Jack was about eight years and nine months old and, depending on his age when he started school, probably in either the fourth or fifth grade.[8]

Their first California home was in Venice, where they rented a small house across the boardwalk from the beach. Dick took a job selling electric robes, that is, electric blankets having a supposed therapeutic effect, on commission. For these Iowans by way of Idaho, the ocean front was an exciting place where they could watch Mack Sennett make his silent comedies. One of these featured a girl behind a big umbrella to which was attached a strong black thread. At the proper time the umbrella was lifted by it, but in the finished movie the umbrella appeared to levitate by itself. Another time Dick walked up town to where a movie was being filmed in a restaurant with Fatty Arbuckle throwing plates and dishes, breaking them with reckless if not furious abandon. Dick was both amused and appalled at the wasteful destruction associated with movie making.

But if the sea provided an attractive beach, it could also present another face. The ocean was not always a good neighbor. One morning the family awakened to the surf pounding at their front steps. Unusually high seas had brought the waves nearly to their front door. Prudence suggested a move farther inland, and by February the family had moved away from the beach into a bigger house. It was there that several things happened. Jack's sister "Chubby" (Dorothy Anne Simplot) was born, Peggy pulled the lever in a fire alarm box, thinking it was a mailbox, and they watched the filming of *The Greatest Show on Earth*, the silent film, not the "talkie" with James Stewart.

It was while they were living in Venice that Jack was one day given a nickel, with which, instead of buying an ice cream cone he bought two newspapers. He promptly converted them into the wherewithal to purchase a supply of the medium, and he found himself on the street in the retail newspaper business. Competition with other boys and threats by streetwise hawkers caused him to seek a safer place to do business—an indoor venue—and all this when he was eight years old.[9]

The residue of capital from this venture Jack came to call his "taw," a term from the game of marbles in which the taw was the shooter, the agent essential for further gain and usually the player's favorite marble, perhaps an "aggie," (agate). From this experience, Jack learned that you don't spend or lose your taw, for then you can't buy any more papers. The knowledge stayed with him all his life, and it became a standard bit of advice with which he inspired countless college graduates in annual commencement addresses.

"Get hold of something," he would say in the passionate tones of an evangelist, "and hang on. Just hang on. If somebody wants it, hang on. It's worth as much to you as it is to anybody who wants it." This bit of wisdom gained from a childhood experience of selling newspapers is one of the profound reminders that life's experiences will teach whoever has the capacity to learn. Jack Simplot has been an apt student in that school.

It is not clear how apt a student he was in the other, which, as Jack recalls, was Washington School. However, it may have been a teacher at this institution in Venice, California, who discovered that he had an unusually fine singing voice. She was so convinced of his talent that she took him home, met his parents, and strongly urged them to see to it that he had voice training.[10]

In the spring of 1918, Dick gave up the selling job, and the Simplots returned to Burley. While Dick worked at building a new house, Dorothy took Bob and the baby up to the dry farm belonging to her sister and brother-in-law, the Schwaeglers. Dick stayed near his work, living in a hotel room and keeping with him Jack, Myrtle, and Peggy, who were in school. That summer trainloads of volunteers and conscriptees left home to enter the service and make the world safe for democracy. Civilians hung effigies of Kaiser Bill from any support strong enough to sustain the weight, ate corn bread, roasted grains of one sort or another to create substitutes for coffee, which they learned to drink without sugar. That rationed item was saved for more important tasks than sweetening coffee. When the Armistice was declared, the Simplots rejoiced along with their Burley neighbors.

However, the siren call of California lured the Simplots back to the Golden State, where they settled on a five-acre chicken ranch near Santa Rosa. Young Jack learned to caddy at a local golf course, earning twenty-five cents per nine hole round plus a twenty-five cent tip.[11] The "ranch" was productive, and the time there was happy. There were plum, apricot, almond, and pear trees to climb and from which to gather produce. The house was large and comfortable; three generations of one family, the Barnetts, had lived in it. Ethel Lorraine Simplot was born in Santa Rosa on November 30, 1919, the second of the children born in California. The family history continues by adding that life there was good with light work and a wonderful climate. Dick improved the place by building a new 1000-capacity hen-house and enclosing the water tank.

But within three years the Burley banks collapsed, and in these institutions Dick had placed his life savings, a considerable loss. In order to save the farms which he had sold but which were not yet paid for, he had to reclaim them, buying them for back taxes against them. The family moved back to Burley in 1922. Sale of the chicken ranch provided him with enough money to regain his property. Before he left California, he told friends there that he would make back what he had lost and return in five years. He made it in four. By that time, however, land values around Santa Rosa had increased significantly. After looking around for a month for property valued similarly to what he had sold, California was abandoned as a place in which to become rooted.

Those four years were a time of hard work, scrimping, and saving. Almost every animal, crop, or activity from which a profit could be made was utilized. Hives of bees produced honey, and the garden produced fruit (including raspberries) and vegetables which were canned or dried. The horseradish had to go through the food grinder to capture its eye-punishing essence before it was canned. The pork was salted, and fat was carefully trimmed off the carcass so that it could be rendered, for lard was the only cooking oil available. Young Jack continued to perfect his capabilities as a farmer, including the essential skills of a teamster. To anticipate the career of this man, it is accurate to say that in his life's work, straddling the twentieth century as it does, he progressed from horse power to cyberspace.

Work on the farm was a consuming thing, at least on a farm run by Charles Richard Simplot. Jack remembers:

> *Hell, I was a man at fourteen. I'd do anything! I farmed, I did all the horse-backing, I did the . . . plowing. I did it all! And I could do it—harness those damned horses and take care of 'em just like I'd been at it for a life-time . . . We had two big teams, and we had a smaller team; we'd run eight to ten head of horses all the time . . . . I learned to work, and the old man . . . by God, we'd run home from school and go to work. I fed the pigs and milked the cows and separated the milk.*
>
> *My mother'd run the cow deal. She was the head milker and she and I* [would do most of it], *and Dad would milk once in a while. My*

sisters never milked. He had about eighteen to twenty cows, and there were always six-seven-eight-ten of 'em [giving milk], *and we had to milk them. He'd get in the wagon and take that cream to town, and I don't know how much he got for it, probably two-three cents a pound, I guess . . . . But I had a good life as a kid 'cause my people had a little money, and our neighbors didn't have any. I mean they were tough, and all around us were . . . Mormons . . .*

The Tollman family—big Mormon family—lived right across the road, and they had fourteen children. . . . And I went over there and stayed overnight . . . and we slept out in the granary, and I remember seeing the bedbugs climbin' up that . . . granary. . . . I went in to breakfast, and I never will forget it: they had a little tub . . . maybe a foot high and a foot and a half across. . . boiled wheat, boiled wheat and milk and that was our breakfast! Took that boiled wheat and put some milk in there and a little sugar. . . . And that was our breakfast . . . . We always had . . . pretty good breakfasts [at home]—*pancakes, eggs. But that was our breakfast.*[12]

One activity which the twelve- or thirteen-year-old lad engaged in was the collection and nurture of "bum" lambs from local sheepmen. In the vocabulary of a sheep outfit, a bum lamb is one that, for whatever reason, does not thrive and appears doomed in the nature of things. Perhaps it was injured at birth, could not compete against a stronger sibling for the mother's milk, or for some other reason seemed destined for a short life. Many of these little creatures could be saved, provided they were given proper care. Sheepmen often made presents of these "bummers" to local children. Jack received his share, and with his mother's help constructed shelters from the wind for them and raised them on bottles. With a good survival rate, he converted the fat and frisky survivors into gold certificates amounting to $80, a considerable amount of paper money for a boy to have. He tells the story this way:

> *I got acquainted with a sheepman, and he had a big bunch of sheep, fella by the name of Pons* [or Ponds]. *He was a big sheepman—Frenchman. And he and my folks . . . were neighbors. I'd go home at night, walk home from school, and he'd give me a bum lamb, and I had twenty-two of these bum lambs. And my mother took the front porch of our house and put quilts around the damn thing and straw on the porch, and we kept those damn lambs. I have to give her all the credit of feeding 'em and seeing that they got fed: she had to feed 'em with a bottle! And these damn lambs, twenty-two of 'em as I remember it, we sold 'em, and we got eighty bucks for 'em.*[13]

At about the age of fourteen, young Simplot possessed another taw.

ChapterThree Notes

1. (Burley, Idaho, 1974) 638.

2. ibid.

3. JRS, 9-16-98, tape 1, side A.

4. (Burley, Idaho, 1974) 638.

5. Jack may have used the wrong term here, for Masons claim to believe in God.

6. JRS, 9-16-98, tape 1, side B.

7. There are differing accounts here. Another version says Mr. Simplot divided his farms into 40-acre units and had several buyers; the money from the sales was placed in various Burley banks. See George Gilder, *The Spirit of Enterprise* (New York: Simon and Schuster, 1984), 25.

8. Jack's birthdate of January 4, 1909, makes the reader wonder whether he started school as a child aged five years and nine months (September 1914) or six years and nine months (September 1915). If the former, he would likely have been a fourth grader; if the latter, a fifth grader. A letter from Esther Wong, Chief Technology Officer, Information 37 Technology Division of the Los Angeles Unified School District, states in response to an inquiry about Jack's attendance there: "Dear Dr. Attebery: We regret to inform you that upon referring to our records, we were unable to establish attendance for John Richard "Jack" Simplot."

9. Hal Bunderson, *Idaho Entrepreneurs* (Boise: Boise State University, 1992) 12.

10. "When I was going to school, I wasn't a [good] student. I was good at [geography]. I knew pretty near all the countries and their capitals, but I never learned to spell, and I never did learn to spell. [on the subject of arithmetic] "Oh yeah, I can get my . . . figures. I was pretty smart at that." JRS interview, 9-16-98, tape 1, side A. As for his singing voice, Esther, Jack's second wife and a trained vocalist, seconds everything the teacher said about Jack's potential: "He has what is called a Wagnerian tenor voice . . . . It's so big! I mean he has that volume . . . that comes from the huge chest . . . . He can harmonize; he has twice as much musical ability as I have. No doubt about it, he would have been wonderful." (2-9-2000) So the world gained a billionaire, and music lost a *heldentenor.*

11. Bunderson, 13.

12. JRS, 9-16-98, tape 1, side A.

13. JRS interview, 9-16-98, tape 2, side A. The spelling of Pons is uncertain. It may be mentioned here that Mr. Simplot's reminiscences develop with great consistency, suggesting that he is in command of his materials and that they are truthful to the facts as he remembers them. He has been interviewed and taped by professional writers in great numbers, for he is good "copy,"but up to this present exception, he has declined to permit his biography to be done. Although every writer must work within the respectable limits of humility, for one's own work is subject to the same laws of verity that operate on all products of the creative impulse, it is nevertheless tempting to point out the mistakes in other works. Some writers, for instance, do not know that gold certificates are not coins, that Mr. Simplot was not the oldest child in the family, and that the chicken ranch was in Santa Rosa, not Venice, California, and that Dick (Charles Richard, Jack's father) died in 1974, not 1979.

Chapter Four

The break . . . and the making of a venture capitalist

Two circumstances of transcendent importance now occur in the life of young—he was about fourteen—John Richard Simplot. They must be contextualized. The first has to do with his education: he finished the eighth grade and to all intents and purposes left school. The second was his utilization of the $80 in gold certificates to buy—speculate on—the warrants with which public school teachers were paid in lieu of checks, for many school districts then had no money in the bank.

There are some astronomic differences between public school education in the teens and twenties and public education now. Whatever school law said about a student remaining in school until reaching a specified age, it is a fact that not all students at that time finished the eighth grade. It had been only recently that an age limit was set, displacing the older requirement that a student finish a certain number of "terms" in order to qualify for a public school diploma, and, in some instances, pass an exit examination. Some school districts could maintain a school for a limited number of terms of instruction during the year, and sometimes the term or terms conflicted with the necessity for the boy or girl to do farm work. The winter term was often the only uninterrupted school session for the entire year, for many youngsters worked in the fields throughout the fall and spring terms. These sometime students were essentially units of production whose availability helped promote, indeed, was essential to, the economic viability of the farm.

Instead of farm life promoting agrarian bliss as Jefferson had envisioned, it often inculcated the most demanding life of toil, occasionally rewarding, often not. And as for a student going on to high school, it may well have been that half or slightly fewer ever aspired to such an intellectual challenge. High school remained just that: a higher form of public education, essentially designed to do two things. The second followed from the first. If the young men and women had been prepared by their high school education to enter college, then it was expected that such a youngster had also been prepared to succeed in the job market. A consequence of this model of public education was that teachers tended to command considerable respect in their communities. Although that respect rarely translated into professional salaries, with regard to psychic income, teacher remuneration was often remarkable.

But Jack Simplot not only left school; he also left home.

American literature is full of examples of young men who find home life intolerable and who "light out for the Territory." American life offers many such examples also. A brief look at sociological theory may be enlightening as to how the Virginian, in Owen Wister's Western classic, responded to too much "older brothering," and how young Lat Evans joined a trail herd moving from eastern Oregon to Montana: "You couldn't figure Pa . . . . So you loved him and you kind of hated him, and you had to get away," is how A. B. Guthrie, Jr. said it in *These Thousand Hills*.[1]

A sociologist whose thinking clarifies the matter is David Riesman. His book *The Lonely Crowd: A Study of the Changing American Character* puts the matter thus:

In an earlier time, people comprising a culture took their sense of direction, gained their identity, and established their values through the tradition of inspiration and leadership provided by an authority figure. He might be an emperor, a king, a high priest, or a mighty war chief. The conformity of its typical members "is insured by their tendency to follow tradition: these I shall term (writes Riesman) *tradition-directed people* and the society in which they live a *society dependent on tradition-direction*." As the Renaissance and the Reformation develop, "conformity is insured by [the tendency of its typical numbers] to acquire early in life an internalized set of goals." This, of course, is an *inner-directed society* made up of *inner-directed people*. The final member of this triad is the society of *other-directed people*, dependent on hints, behavior patterns, and the expectations of contemporaries—others—in the establishment of social character.[2]

In his search for a model or metaphor that will

clarify his meaning, Riesman discovers two that are quite remarkably apt. It is as if the individuals comprising the inner-directed society have gyroscopes near the center of their being, and the values, attitudes, and work habits of the leaders of this society energize or wind up the gyroscopes of the young and set them in motion. Those familiar with this mechanical marvel of a toy—or something more serious, like the guidance system of a torpedo—know that the little machine behaves almost as if it were sentient. It can progress along a straight line, it can "walk" a stretched string, it can encounter various obstacles and challenges, but as long as its center—its whirling central motor—is moving, the entire object will find its way. With human beings, of course, the center is spiritual or emotional or perhaps even intellectual. Thus those life experiences that appear to challenge, threaten, or subvert traditional values are bumps in the road or detours, for the individual never really abandons what has been internalized.[3] On the other hand, because they lack any central core value, other-directed individuals constantly send and receive signals from others, who are doing the same thing. For them, the radar set is an appropriate metaphor.[4]

One of the charcteristics of the inner-directed person is that because of his independent cast of mind he will often be in conflict with the very source(s) of his directedness. Thus he may—often does—rebel against father or grandfather or older brothers and strike out on his own, but because his gyroscope works efficiently and was long ago set in motion by those same representatives of authority, he never divagates very widely from their patterns. This consistency, however, must not be confused with slavish imitation. Instead, what prevails is something very like what folklorists call "dynamic variation." The creative and imaginative forces of the individual's mind receive the values from authority, but his insistence upon his own way of doing results in a meld of the old and the new, the transmitted and the modification of it, the "public" and the private.

And so Jack Simplot had to light out on his own. His words put the matter well:

> *And when I left home, my mother had kept the money* [from the sale of the fat lambs], *and she gave me four $20 gold certificates. You know, you used to get gold certificates. Instead of $20 greenbacks they were $20 gold certificates—same price, same thing. And that's what got me started. And this is a true . . . story. . . . Anyway, I put that $80 in my pocket, and of course I was scared of losing it or somebody'd hold me up or steal it or some damn thing. Well, I finally had to go to the bank, and I put it up as collateral at the bank, and I was staying at a boarding house. . . . I own the damn thing today. . . . I finally bought it from the old lady. She had, oh, about eight schoolteachers living in this apartment house: a dollar a day and board and room* [at the] *Enyeart Hotel.*
>
> *And she had two daughters. I wasn't much of a lady's man . . . . hell, I was only fourteen. I thought I was doing damn good to make a*

> *living. I took this . . . money that I got from these sheep, and I went in and got acquainted with my banker . . . . These eight-ten schoolteachers . . . weren't paid with money; they were paid with scrip* [interest-bearing warrants], *and I could buy that scrip for about fifty cents on the dollar. Nobody'd buy the . . . scrip so I'd buy these . . . and take 'em into the bank, and he'd give me full credit for the damn things. They paid four percent. It wasn't a lotta money, but it was enough money to make some money. I'd buy that scrip every month when* [they got paid]. *They had to pay their board bill . . . . Damn board bill was about half their* [salary]. *Tough. You talk about tough times; they were tough! Tough, boy! But I accumulated a few hundred dollars, and I made some money.*[5]

By the time he was fourteen years old, Jack was on his own. He was making money, and he had learned that money will make money. To compare him with another entrepreneur, by the time John D. Rockefeller was sixteen years old he was pounding the streets of Cleveland looking for a job.[6] Jack's interior mechanism, his gyroscope of inner-directedness, had been thoroughly energized and set in motion by his father, for Charles Richard was a hard worker and a stern taskmaster. More than that, he was a careful and highly skilled worker. Except for fishing and hunting, there was no time for play, which, after all, did not produce anything, whereas hunting and fishing paid off in bounty for the table. Moreover, there was the abiding lesson of thrift. The childhood period of Jack

Simplot's life ended; the adolescent time began.

When David Riesman described the psychological makeup of the type of personality he calls inner-directed, he might well have had Charles Richard Simplot and his son in mind. Riesman says, for example, "The inner-directed parent . . . asks more of his child, just as he asks more of himself"[7] and again, "the tradition-directed child propitiates his parents; the inner-directed child fights or succumbs to them." [8] Fights or succumbs: John Richard was not about to succumb, so he fought.

We do not know exactly what happened when young Jack left home. No one was on hand with a tape recorder to catch the language of the event. We are told that young Jack had had enough, that he could not take time off from work to watch a basketball game or waste a moment shagging fly balls or do anything unconnected with the financial success of the family. *Origins of the J. R. Simplot Company*, an official corporation publication, says simply, "At age 14, frustrated by the overbearing demeanor of his father, Jack dropped out of school and left home."[9] In the written record, there is no evidence of physical abuse, nor do audio tape recordings even hint at such matters.

Domiciled at the Enyeart Hotel, a Declo boarding house, Jack, as we have seen, capitalized on, or actually created a market for, school district warrants with which teachers were paid in lieu of cash. He got acquainted with the local banker. He equipped himself with a second hand Model T pickup with a Ruckstell axle and undertook any kind of day laborer's job that would bring in cash . . . field work, riprapping irrigation canals, sorting potatoes. . . any and all of these would help preserve his taw, what those four $20 gold certificates and the teachers' warrants had gained for him. Then in what can be seen as a foreshadowing of the Simplot success strategy, he made a bold move and came out of it redolent with the sweet smell of success.

There seems to be no such thing as a Simplot formula for achievement, but if there were, if it were possible to reduce all the strategies employed over time to bring about his triumphs, these strategies can be found to consist of timeliness, hard work, imagination or creativity in seeing what other eyes failed to note, and the conviction that the undertaking will or can be made to work. A synonym is optimism or faith. One other quality Simplot had in spades.

Of all these, timeliness is the most problematical. Somewhere Ralph Waldo Emerson has said, "Shallow minds believe in luck. . . . Strong men believe in cause and effect." How can it be known just when the crisis moment has arrived? Is it a matter left exclusively in the hands of fortune? It seems fair to suggest that judgment and a sense of history are extremely important in this matter of timeliness. With respect to judgment, we are dealing with another imponderable. We recognize judgment as having been strong or weak when we see its results in operation. We incline to believe that there may be something genetic about it, for a stockman noted for his ability to guess an animal's weight within one pound, a freight car load of livestock with an error of less than three pounds per animal, can be shown to have produced sons with similar talents.

This same capacity of exercising judgment may be found in the farmer who can estimate accurately the tonnage expected from a crop of alfalfa, the number of bushels to the acre a crop of wheat may be expected to produce from a given field or fields, and just the right time to cut the hay or harvest the grain. The sense of history enters the equation as experience upon experience informs the sense of judgment. Cattle have looked this way before and have weighed such and such; hay was cut just this time before in particular reference to the maturity of the blossom. These experiences meld into a complex pattern which then articulates with the capacity for making a reasoned judgment. With the right kind of intelligence, a few experiences count for more than does the repetition of a hundred. It is qualitative, not quantitative. But the capacity must be there. If it is, then the person so blessed will make the right decision in a timely fashion.

Young Jack Simplot knew that markets for farm goods experience wide and sometimes wild shifts. Beef, lamb, and hog prices go down and up and down. The stock market pendulum, indeed, all pendulums whose swings mark the changes inherent in whatever it is they are thought to measure, is highly mobile. In 1922 the market for hogs hit the bottom. Jack's judgment told him it was the right time to buy, and so he bought hogs. That the break with his father was neither terminal nor vicious was signaled by Dick's willingness to assist in the building of pens and the construction of vats to be used in the making of food for the hundreds of hogs Jack had purchased and in permitting his son to transform a corner of his farm into a place where hogs could be raised and fattened.

Jack had an idea about that, too. Cull potatoes were available; they could be utilized by hogs if the starches were first broken down by cooking. What might be added to the potatoes? By themselves, they sustained life but did not provide sufficient nutrients to make the animals gain weight. What about meat? Where could he obtain meat cheaply? Why not harvest the wild horses? "Were there a lot of them in that country?" he was asked.

> *Oh, there was a hundred head of wild horses in that bunch, I think. And I killed a couple with some brands on 'em, too . . . . But I went out and settled with* [the guy] *who had some horses running loose. Sold the hides. You'd get a couple of bucks for a horsehide, and of course I didn't take the whole hide. I'd just cut him around the neck and I didn't take the legs. I sawed off the legs. Then I put a rope on top . . . of the thing. Then I'd put a big spike in the ground to hold him, and then I'd back up the car and jerk it I could jerk a hide off in nothin' flat. . . . Then I'd take the quarters and throw 'em in the truck and go get another one. It took about two horses every cook* [batch].
>
> *Yeah, I was in my teens. . . but I had an idea and it worked, and my dad, naturally, he helped me. He helped me build the damn thing*

> *and he knew. He was a carpenter, and we built good sheds, and I put it on a creek* [pron. "crick"] *where the pigs could get all the water they needed. And I had to build some pens so they could sleep. And hogs, you know, . . . won't mess up their nest. They're smart; they won't mess up their nests.*
>
> *I didn't care about what color or what they were, but they were a mixed bunch. . . . I sold the big ones as I bought 'em—took the big ones to town and you could get a couple dollars for a big sow, and the boars . . . were hard to sell. Wasn't the market, just no market. Then I'd buy the little pigs. That's what I really wanted, and I imagine I was paying a dollar a head for the little pigs. That's how I got most of 'em.*
>
> *It was a venture that worked. But I had to get some help before I got through. I hired a couple more kids to help. We had to cut brush to cook the . . . potatoes; then the big job was to get 'em outa the cooker. They're red hot, you know, and you gotta get in there and shovel 'em out and set 'em out so they'll cool a day and then maybe turn them once to get the heat out of 'em. Potatoes (cooked whole) and horsemeat: that's what I fed 'em.*[10]

Jack was right about meat and potatoes as a nourishing diet for pigs. He was right about the market, too. It turned and as it did so, Jack's worthless livestock—700 or so hogs—became worth seven cents a pound, netting him $7,800, a princely quantity of money in that era. What had the venture cost him?

Practically nothing but work, although it was hard work. Quarters of horse meat, bone in, weigh a considerable amount, and lifting them onto a pickup bed required great strength. He may have slaughtered half a hundred horses, so ammunition for his father's 32/40 Winchester (he thought it was) was a consideration. But no, that cost and the cost of gasoline for his pickup truck came out of the $2 or so he got for the horsehides. What about his labor? Farmers have often been said to charge an insufficient amount for their labor, if, indeed, in their final accounting they charge anything for it. But those costs go with the territory.

The venture with the pigs is a casebook illustration of the way Simplot's mind worked. Optimism: he had to believe in positive results. The willingness to work: tossing quarters of horse meat about and stirring and shovelling the thick stew establish his willingness to labor and labor hard. His judgment insisted that the market would shift and would do so in a timely manner. All these components create an attractive package, one that stood Jack Simplot in good stead as he ascended the ladder of success. Now he had a taw of considerable weight. And now he must capitalize upon it. With the $7,800 he bought work horses, harnesses for them, farm implements, and seeds of various kinds. He leased land and listened to good advice. He was on his way, and he was only in his early teens.

Chapter Four Notes

1. (New York: Pocket Books, 1956) 2-3

2. (New Haven and London: Yale University Press, 1961) 8. See Chapter 1, "Character and Society," especially pp. 24-36.

3. *Crowd*, 16.

4. *Crowd*, 25.

5. JRS interview, 9-16-98, tape 2, side A.

6. Ron Chernow, *Titan: The Life of John D. Rockefeller, Sr.* (New York: Random House, 1998) 44.

7. *Crowd* , 42.

8. *Crowd*, 52.

9. J. R. Simplot Company (1997) 5.

10. JRS interview, 9-16-98, tape 1, side A. Most Westerners seemed to accept Arthur Miller's "Misfits" for what it was: a half truth about Western matters by an Easterner who either did not know what he was talking about or, knowing, was content to exploit those matters in the interests of art. It is common knowledge among Westerners that wild horse herds had been and would be for some time fair game for hunters to capture and ship to cities where they would be transformed into pet and chicken feed. Even worn-out draft animals were often sold for "chicken feed," the term meaning "nearly worthless," as well as literal "commercial food for chickens and pets." What a different vision of reality from the sentimental portraiture of catching wild horses that would then be sold, domesticated, and transformed exclusively into children's ponies. It is on that sentimental untruth that the moral issue of the *Misfits* rests.

Chapter Five

Certified seed

With horses, equipment, and an eagerness that can be imagined, young Simplot was ready. Now he needed land, not to buy but to rent. Accordingly, he leased 120 acres from a neighbor named Kate Maggart Walker and an additional forty acres from Kate's brother, Lindsay, giving him a quarter of a section of irrigated land, a good-sized piece of property for one man to work.[1] Along with the Maggart land came Maggart advice, and that was to raise potatoes using only certified seed. According to Simplot the seed is,

> *certified by a state agency, and you can only certify it through your agricultural college. . . .* [But] *instead of buying certified seed during the '30s, I accumulated thirty-three potato sheds between Vale, Oregon, and Idaho Falls [Idaho]. Up and down the Snake River Valley. And I got my farmers to plant ten sacks of certified seed for their seed next year. "Keep the*

sprouts off," I told them, "and plant the first of June, late, and dig early and put it away for your seed for next year." And that was a big step in the right direction to make a better potato. And then we learned from my old farmer [Maggart]. *He wouldn't let us put potatoes on any ground but hay ground that had been in alfalfa three-four years. That was his system, and it worked. We got a better potato, a better crop and more tonnage.*[2]

But the accumulation of potato packing sheds was still in the future, as young Jack set himself up to be a farmer. Whatever reservations may have been held by Jack's landlords about doing business with a minor, they were quickly dispelled. Here was a youth, well-connected and with a solid family—never mind his living on his own—who, moreover, had his own money. There is no more forceful argument for probity, reliability, and good citizenship. Simplot remembers:

I farmed 120 acres for three years, but I happened to rent this farm from the best potato grower in Idaho. He got to be an alcoholic, and his family kicked him out, and that's why he rented me this ranch. I knew his son, and I got acquainted with him through his son, and he just rented me this 120 acres, and I raised him good crops, and we were partners on the crops, but he was a good friend of mine. I took care of him. I hustled that two pints of moonshine he had to have every day to live. He had to have it. And I took him to California a couple of times to see his sister, and I had to get him into town, and I had to hustle a bootlegger and buy him—this was during Prohibition—two pints of booze to keep this old boy alive. And it taught me one of the greatest lessons I had—and he'd smoke these damn cigarettes . . . . My dad smoked a pipe, and I just hated the goddamn thing. He'd light up that pipe and I'd get out of the house." [3]

This, one remembers, was that post-World War I segment of time often called the jazz age, the roaring twenties, or, as Frederick Lewis Allen denominates it in *Only Yesterday*, the Decade of Bad Manners.[4] It is appropriate to take a brief look at the social context of Jack Simplot's novitiate as a farmer.

Simplot tells us that he left home when he was fourteen. Yes, his mother hated it, and the family was upset, but he couldn't get along with his father, so what else was there to do? This would have been in 1922 or 1923. If two years are allowed for his working at what jobs he could find and for his venture with the hogs, then he was ready to begin farming on leased property in 1925. This went on for at least three years, or until 1928. Everybody can connect the following year, 1929, with one of the terrible spasms in American economic life.

Frederick Lewis Allen suggests that the most violent public social issues of the 1920s vibrated between two als: alcohol and Al Capone.[5] In his whimsical manner, Allen summarizes the impact on the American social fabric of the Eighteenth Amendment and the

Volstead Act which provided for its enforcement. And it's all there: tommy guns, massacres, rum-runnning, huge fortunes illegally amassed, an appalling abandonment of good sense, good morality, and, in many cases, good government.

But there are other indices of social behavior that can suggest the energy and the tempo of the twenties. Take, for example, the striking increase in the number of radios, their parts and accessories, manufactured for the public. In 1922, sales amounted to $60 million; in 1925, $430 million; in 1929, $842 million![6] The last figure represents an increase over the 1922 figure of 1,400 percent, but it is not just the arithmetic of the increase that engages the student of social change. Even more interesting is the fact that Americans were buying instruments of communication, the means through which information, news, music and other forms of entertainment were becoming almost commonplace. Keosauqua, Iowa, and Kendrick, Idaho, could hear the same cultural products, and neither place need feel the stigma of provincialism. For another example, the popularity enjoyed by the movies was phenomenal, and the fortunes amassed by actors, studios, directors, and producers were immense.

Equally significant was the social/moral tone reflected by the silver screen. Cocktails and cigarettes consumed by consumately attractive figures in exquisitely designed settings modified American notions of diligence, sobriety, personal morality, and hard work. Allen writes that "attendance at the motion-picture houses of 'Middletown' during a single month (December 1923) amounted to four and a half times the entire population of the city . . . as men, women, and children, rich and poor, went to the movies at an average rate of better than once a week!"[7] A final example is the automobile, to which Allen devotes a substantial part of his Chapter 7, "Coolidge Prosperity." It is the Ford car that Allen finds significant, not the Model T, the "tin lizzie" of pioneer vintage, but the enclosed Model A: "If any sign had been needed of the central place which the automobile had come to occupy in the mind and heart of the average American, it was furnished when the Model A Ford was brought out in December 1927. . . . It was one of the great events [of the year]."[8] Since automobiles achieve gender through rhetorical attribution rather than through sexual characteristics—ships, also, and other items too numerous to mention—cars are inevitably "she." Thus in those days, numberless original, imaginative, and highly creative young men denominated their portable courting parlors "Henrietta," feminizing the product of the great manufacturer and creating a pattern for their successors fortunate enough to find a Model A Ford in their future in the '30s and '40s.

And did farmers share in this spectacular growth and these remarkable profits? Allen writes that "mighty few farmers could get so much as a fingerhold upon [the prosperity bandwagon]."[9] Then, citing the general economic upswing (the aforementioned radios a case in point), Allen asks, "Was this Coolidge prosperity real? The farmers did not think so."[10]

Nevertheless, with few exceptions balance sheets of corporate income, wages, and profits and losses established clearly the fact that Americans were in the money; "between 1922 and 1927, the purchasing power of American wages increased at the rate of more than two percent annually. And during the three years between 1924 and 1927 alone there was a leap from seventy-five to 283 in the number of Americans who paid taxes on incomes of more than a million dollars a year."[11]

On his rented property in Idaho, Jack Simplot and Clarence Hayden, his hired man—he could now afford steady hired help—labored and hoped and labored some more. They planted, dug, sorted, and sacked potatoes. They planted grain, both barley and wheat, dry beans, and hay; they bound, hauled, and threshed the grain; they harvested the beans; they cut, raked, and stacked the hay. Additional help was hired as necessary. The livestock did well. But there was always the driving necessity to increase his income, so in the summer of 1926 Jack hooked up with a neighbor and friend named Carl Olsen and a cousin named Gale Haxby to work in a sawmill on the Oregon coast. Jack Simplot tells it this way:

> *This Carl Olsen and I went to Oregon; we hoboed over there . . . caught rides . . . and I knew this cousin of mine* [Gale Haxby] *. . . was working in a sawmill out on the coast. And he takes us out there, and we both go to work in this sawmill. And* [Gale] *joined the National Guard. He was older than I was. He came to us two and said, "We need more people to go on our summer outing. They take 'em out and*

train 'em for two weeks.

"If you guys want to, we can enlist you in the army." I think it was two or three or four weeks, so I joined the National Guard, and my buddy, well, both of us kinda filled the numbers. Hell, I was still a teenager, but I told 'em I was twenty-one or whatever the hell you had to do to get in the army [actually eighteen with parental consent]. . . . *Anyway, it was a helluv'n experience. I was there for two-three weeks, and I put in the damnedest two weeks. All they did was* [march] *and I was marchin' with guys who'd been in the army for years . . . and finally I got the lesson, and I thought Geez, if I ever get outa this thing I'll never go back into it because they get ya up in the morning and run ya around and up and down in that hardpack, stickery damn stuff, but anyway it was a helluv'n experience. . . . Anyway, I got out of that deal . . . my dad . . . I don't know how he got me out of it . . . .*[12] *We stayed one winter in Springfield, Oregon, I remember. I went to school there in Springfield, for a short time. I don't know how long it was. And when the weather broke, Dad headed back to the farm, and I went with him.*[13]

Several bits of information require comment. Carl Olsen probably did not spell his name the Swedish way: Olson. *Declo—My Town My People* uses this form.[14] This summer experience with the National Guard can be accurately dated by virtue of a company photograph in Simplot's possession. He was a member of "C" company, 162nd Infantry, that met at Camp Jackson, Medford, Oregon, in the summer of 1926. He was seventeen.

The closing four or five years of the 1920s witnessed considerable interest in this thing called the "National Guard." An act promulgated by Ohio Congressman Charles W. Dick in 1903 had been the beginning of its reformation and modernization. This legislation replaced the Militia Acts of May 2 and May 8, 1792, declaring that the National Guardsmen would be the "Organized Militia" with the rest of the manpower in the states comprising the "Reserve Militia," an expression which preceded the phrase "military manpower pool," used by the Selective Service. Put simply, the legislation for the draft of World War I and the selective service of World War II derived from the Dick Act.[15]

The next legislation affecting the Guard was enacted as the National Defense Act of 1916, the most all-encompassing military legislation in our history up to that time, and much of it is still operative.[16] The Act defined the word "Militia" ("all able-bodied citizens of the United States and all other able-bodied males who have or shall have declared their intentions to become citizens of the United States, who shall be more than 18 years of age and younger than 45, and said Militia shall be divided into three classes: the National Guard, the Naval Militia, and the Unorganized Militia," the last group comprising the pool of the draft eligible.[17]

The final piece of legislation advancing the reformation and modernization of the National Guard was the National Defense Act of June 4, 1920, which with minor changes, was in force until the mobilization of 1940-41.[18] Among its various provisions—the peace time establishment would have three elements: the Regular Army, the National Guard, and the Organized Reserve, the predecessor of today's U.S. Army Reserve—Section 10 bears upon enlisted men, among whom in 1926 was Private John Richard Simplot. This section stipulated that enlisted men were to receive one day's pay at their grade for each full participation at drills "duly ordered" but for no more than eight in any month and sixty in one year.[19] In addition to the expectation of sixty drill periods a year, there was the fifteen-day summer field camp.[20]

There is no reason to think that the Oregon Guard was in any way exceptional. It may have been typical in conducting its business in a somewhat casual manner, permitting seventeen-year-olds to enlist for summer encampment and then allowing them to "de-enlist," although we do not know how persuasive Dick Simplot was in reclaiming his son. On the other side of the equation, there must have been a climate in America in 1926 which encouraged young men to enlist in the Guard. To describe that climate and then to account for it require some reflection. It was clearly a climate of patriotism. Young men uncovered when the flag—"Old Glory"—passed by in parades. Young men stood at attention when they were expected to do so in the presence of the flag as patriotic sympathies were engaged. Young men would willingly enlist to serve their country's cause. If *The Star Spangled Banner* had not yet been elevated to the status of the national anthem, there were plenty of other singable tunes and slogans to which they attended seriously: *Columbia the Gem of the Ocean*, with its *Three cheers for the Red, White, and Blue* is still a stirring song. And there were others. To account for this spirit is not difficult.

Many of the young men spoken of here were too young to have served in the Great War, but they remembered it, and the magical names from that struggle fairly haunted them: the Western Front, Chateau-Thierry, the Meuse Argonne, Belleau Wood, the Rainbow Division, the AEF. Our Boys! Over There! The world safe for democracy! Americans did not believe they confused jingoism-chauvinism with patriotism. And besides all this, had not America just recently—within the last six years—survived red scares, an imminent police strike, a bomb blast near Wall Street, and the anarchy of Sacco and Vanzetti? [21]

To a patriotic lad in 1926, the National Guard undoubtedly appeared to be the best organization through which his patriotism could be channeled and the insidious threats to the American Way of Life successfully countered. In view of the agricultural depression, farm kids must have found the slight income from monthly drills and summer encampment alluring indeed, provided they could somehow arrange transportation to town to meet those obligations. In any case, that year saw the National Guard represented in twenty-one Oregon counties with 185 officers, three warrant officers, and 2,924 enlisted men for a total of 3,111 men, the maximum then allowed by the War Department. [22]

After leaving the National Guard, Jack worked

wherever he could find a job until mid-year, at which time he studied at Springfield High School, attended classes briefly, then returned to Idaho with his dad, who had endured all the Oregon moisture he could bear. His experience at Springfield was typical of his sporadic and abortive attempts to achieve a high school education. Over the years, Jack has made no secret of his limited education. He finished the eighth grade and made at least two attempts to negotiate high school. One of these was at Springfield, the other was in his hometown of Declo. *Declo—My Town, My People* puts it this way: "Cliff Darrington said that Jack sat in front of him in study hall at Declo High and, toward spring, he hadn't come to school for several days and Cliff asked him why. Jack said, 'Those fellows are paying me four dollars a day for sorting spuds. I can't afford to go to school.'"[23]

It is with the sorting of potatoes that Jack Simplot's life turned another corner, and to that vegetable, to that anything-but-glamorous subject, we turn, after a brief glimpse at another manifestation of the hobo in Simplot. His own words catch the flavor of youth and adventure:

> *He and I* [were] *pitchin' bundles . . . and I said "Let's go to Canada. They're gettin' five dollars a day up there [for what] we're doing here. . . ." So we struck out on foot. . . went into Pocatello. That's an honest-to God story. We got on a train outa Pocatello. . . first time I was ever hoboin', and we got on a freight train, and the thing went to Yellowstone Park. We thought*

we were goin' to Butte, Montana! . . . . And we had to come back to Pocatello on the same damn train. . . . We got another train and went to Butte . . . . From there we went to Moosejaw, Canada, hoboin'.

We stayed a day or two in town [at a boarding house] *run by this woman. Then we went out and got a job, and they paid us five dollars a day. We worked there a week or two, bindin' this wheat and thrashin'. And I never got back to pay my board bill for the couple of nights we stayed there in somebody's house. Then it got colder, and when we were comin' back to town, there was a train goin' west and Bill* [Gibson] *said, 'Let's get on that train and get out of this damn country.' I never did pay that board bill, and it's bothered me all my life. I beat that woman outa two-three nights board bill 'cause I never got back to pay her. Course I didn't have her name and didn't have an address. But I got into Butte, Montana, and I said, "This is a tough world out there . . . boxcar, sleepin' in a boxcar!" So I went in and bought me a big, thick pair of underwear, thickest I could find. And I had some money—I had two hundred dollars—and I taped it on my leg. I said, "Well, you travel with a bunch of bums." I never will forget that.*

We [went] *clear across Canada, went into Vancouver. Rode the rails! We got up there on the train, and if you couldn't find an open boxcar, you had to ride on top! I never got under one, but some of those hobos got under the damn train and rode on those braces. I never did that, but I did the boxcars. You take one and open it up, and if there's a place to sleep, why you got in there and shut the door. That was one helluva ride that I took from there to Vancouver. And damn near went to Alaska. I was too young, but he* [Bill Gibson] *was old enough to go up there. He could get a job at a fishery someplace in Alaska. But it was the fall of the year—winter was comin' on. . . . I was about fifteen or sixteen. He was about twenty.*[24]

Although dates often prove to be less than totally reliable in oral history, it would be safe to say that Jack was indeed probably fifteen or sixteen. However, there is no question as to the authenticity of the events. What happened is true; exactly when it happened is unclear.

When common sense combines with good fortune, the blend can be stunning. When, for instance, in Jack's teens a business visit to the Cassia County Courthouse prompted Sheriff Pace to say to him, "Jack, I'm gonna sell some land in the Raft River Valley. Why don't you give me a bid?" Simplot continues the story:

I didn't pay much attention to it, and then I got to thinking. He went out on the courthouse steps and hollered up and down the street that he was going to sell this land in the Raft River Valley, and I thought, hell, I'll give him a bid, so I went out and and I bid him fifty cents an

> *acre, twenty years to pay for it, five percent down, four percent interest. And he sold me eighteen thousand acres in the Raft River Valley!. . . . I just took a gamble. I mean I was in my teens, fella, and I thought, hell, I'll just get me some land, and I did.*[25]

As to the corner turned in his life, once again the name of Lindsay Maggart surfaces, the man who insisted that Jack plant only certified seed potatoes. Two years after the National Guard summer encampment, Jack and Lindsay bought a mechanical potato sorter, each paying half ($127 apiece). Run by electricity, the sorter's important feature was a moving conveyer belt that carried unsorted potatoes dumped on one end past two lines of sorters, one on either side of the belt. The efficiency of the contrivance was remarkable, for it presented a steadily moving quantity of potatoes to the crew that sorted them as the tubers passed by. They could be sorted on any basis the boss chose: size, conformation, condition with respect to health, or any other basis desired. It was, obviously, a big improvement over a stationary table of potatoes from which the sorters would have to sort out both good and bad potatoes. With the conveyer belt, only bad or undesirable (cull) potatoes had to be removed because the machine took care of the good ones. Sorters' attention was now concentrated, and a greater volume of the tubers could pass through their field of attention. With the addition of "spreaders," the belt nudges the potatoes around, allowing multiple viewing and checking as they pass by several sorters.[26]

Sorting his own and then Maggart's potatoes, Simplot found other customers in the highly productive Snake River Valley. Eventually, Maggart cautioned Simplot about sorting potatoes for competitors and thus being unable to sort for Maggart's friends. Cautions led to demands and strong differences of opinion at which point Simplot suggested the expedient of tossing a silver dollar for full ownership of the device. Fortune smiled and he won.

From that event in 1928, Simplot began to expand, utilizing the building skills of master carpenter Cliff Simons, who constructed potato cellars, and in 1930 the bookkeeping-office management skills of Burdell Curtis, until he had a string of potato packing sheds extending from Idaho Falls, Idaho, to Jamieson, Oregon.[27] He seemed on the way to becoming a contractor-freshpacker-shipper as he added onions to his fresh pack activities, under the label of Simplot Produce Company.[28] Simplot would probably never refer to potatoes and onions as "inferior good," a term economists would use. He knew, however, that these items were affordable by folk whose incomes shrank during the Depression, and his common sense told him that people would have to turn to cheap sources of nourishment (inferior good).[29] You can't go wrong supplying people with nutrition they can afford.

Chapter Five Notes

1. Origins, 7.

2. JRS, 4- 8-99, tape 1, side A.

3. JRS, 9-16-98, tape 1, side A. 57

4. (New York: Bantam Books, 1931) 85.

5. Allen, Only Yesterday , 174. Chapter Ten which is so titled.

6. Allen, *Only Yesterday*, 116.

7. Allen, *Only Yesterday*, 118.

8. Allen, *Only Yesterday,* 114-115. For an incisive, trenchant, one-paragraph analysis of changes in the courtship practices of young America, see especially p. 70 of this superb social history.

9. Allen, 113.

10. Allen, 118.

11. Ibid.

12 JRS, 9-16-98, tape 2, side A.

13 An e-mail communication from Cherie Kistner, Communications Specialist for the Springfield Public Schools, dated 1/27/99, reads as follows: "Our records custodian found a Jack Simplot, age 17, enrolled as a sophomore in Springfield High School in January, 1927--but only attended one day--then the book indicates the student was dropped--no indication of a transfer to any other school."

14 Declo--My Town, My People, 639. Company Muster Rolls of the Oregon National Guard spell it "Olsen." Military spelling is usually reliable, especially after the Civil War.

15 Jim Dan Hill, *The Minute Man in Peace and War: A History of the National Guard* (Harrisburg, Pennsylvania, 1964) 187.

16 Hill, *Minute Man*, 221.

17 Hill, *Minute Man*, 222.

18. Hill, *Minute Man*, 314.

19. ibid.

20. Hill, *Minute Man*, 347.

21. See in this connection Allen, *Only Yesterday*, Chapter Three, "The Big Red Scare," pp.31-61.

22. Twentieth Biennial Report of The Addjutant General of the State of Oregon, 1925-1926.

23 *Declo--My Town, My People*, 639.

24 JRS, 10-22-98, tape 1, side A.

25 JRS, 9-16-98, tape 1, side A.

26 JRS, 9-16-98, tape 1, side A.

27Michael V. Woodhouse, e-mail, 7/27/ 99.

28 About Cliff Simons and his cellars, Simplot said: "He was a great guy. When I was first started, he was an expert on building cellars . . . . Simons . . . kept these log poles, and he'd size them and shape them right there so all you had to do was set 'em up. And then we loaded the poles in the box- car and send 'em down to where we were goin' to build the cellar. . . . They were 300 feet long and 60 feet wide. I remember that, and we could get our whole cellar in one boxcar. [Question: What did you use for insulation? Straw? Dirt?] Put down barbed wire, old wire, then we put straw, then we put dirt--covered 'em with dirt. And they had air vents in 'em. . . . I'd get the farmers to bring (the potatoes) in off the farms and put 'em in these cellars, and then I'd sort 'em all winter and sack 'em up. . . . [Question: Take your sorting crews down into the cellars?] We had electricity in all the cellars. And [the operation] had an office, and I built one in Declo and Paul, and then I went to Murtaugh, then I went to Kimberly, and then I went to Jerome, and I built cellars and started into the potato business. . . . We had sorting machines at each station, and I had somebody buying and selling potatoes. During the 30s I accumulated thirty-three potato sheds from Idaho Falls to . . . Jamieson [Oregon]. And I got big in the potato business. I got to be, I guess, one of the biggest shippers in Idaho.10-15-98, Tape 1, side A.

29 Karen Simkins, *A Chronology of the J. R. Simplot Company,* August 1993, 5.

30. George Gilder, *The Spirit of Enterprise* (New York: Simon and Schuster, 1984) 30.

Chapter Six

Courtship and marriage

In December 1931, Jack Simplot and Ruby Rosevear were married in Ontario, Oregon, from which eastern Oregon town they went on their honeymoon, staying at the princely Hotel Baker their first night. How that marriage came about deserves telling. Its dissolution in 1960 is also part of the life story of the subject of this book.

It may be said to have begun with the Kellogg twins, a pair of charmers from Jack's schoolboy days, on one of whom he had his eye.

> *This little gal right here* [looking at a photograph]. . . *I went to school with her up to the eighth grade. And I kinda had my eye on her. I went down and took her out in an airplane here in Boise and it was maybe . . early thirties. Oh, no . . . I got married in 1930* [actually 1931], *so it had to be before then. But they went to school, the Kellogg twins, and they went*

clear through school, and they'd come in just like they'd come out of a [band] *box every day. I guess the old man had a little money; he was a gambler, made money . . . in the pool halls and pickin' up suckers. They had a big Nash car, and I can remember him goin' by our place to get to Burley every day, and he went in and played poker all day, and I d'know . . . . He must've made some money. . . . They sold their ranch, and his wife was a helluva gal. She raised these two kids, and she kept them spotless . . . . He never worked; he hired every thing done, but he was a good poker player . . . didn't smoke or drink . . . but he was a good poker player. Made a living at it, and that was a tough time in the early days.*[1]

As Jack leafed through his album, another photograph surfaced.

There's Frances Kellogg again. This is the little gal I had my eye on, and I guess I thought she was about it . . . . I took her up in an airplane here in Boise. I was in [my] *teens. She went to St. Margaret's, she and her sister, and I brought a fella by the name of Tom Alexander . . . . First time I'd ever been up in an airplane. It was one of those* [with] *two seats in front and one in the back with the pilot in it, and you had to put on goggles . . . 'cause you were right in back of the propellor. She brought another gal for Tom Alexander, and it was the gal I* [later] *married."*[2]

The "gal" was Ruby Rosevear of Glenns Ferry, Idaho. About a year younger than the Kellogg twins, she, too, had left her hometown for Boise and the attractions of the girls' school sponsored by the Episcopal Church, St. Margaret's Hall, which was to become Boise Junior College. She and the twins became fast friends, and when they chose to pursue their higher education at Albion Normal, Ruby, too, decided that was where she wished to go.

Situated in a valley about eight miles above Declo, the little town of Albion is one of the jewels of the southern Idaho mountains, behind the foothills just before the main ascent up 10,000-plus-foot Mt. Harrison. Later called Southern Idaho College of Education (and still later closed by an economy-minded legislature and chief executive), Albion Normal was a two-year training institution for teachers, inexpensive and attractive to young folk of the Twin Falls area, what is now called Magic Valley. It was a counterpart of Lewiston Normal (North Idaho College of Education), which survived the economies of state government to become eventually Lewis-Clark State College. Normal schools were a nationwide movement by teachers' colleges which sought to "normalize" teacher training by providing a standard if not completely uniform curriculum. According to Simplot:

> *As soon as she* [Frances] *got in Albion Normal, she found her another guy somehow or other. So I went up there to see her; she had got her roommate—her roommate was my wife* [to be]—*to go with me.*[3]

It could have been scripted in Hollywood—arranged blind dates, an airplane ride, a roommate substitute who proved more attractive than the original.

The Rosevears of Glenns Ferry, of Cornish descent, were people of substance, owning wholly or in part the local butcher shop, the lumber yard, and a hardware store. They could afford to send their eighth grade daughter to St. Margaret's Hall in remote Boise. There is some indication, too, that Ruby might profit from supervision other than her mother's: "My mother thought that I didn't bend to the rules like I should, and I could go to a girls' school."[4] She was a student there (a boarding student as opposed to a day student) for the next five years, eighth through twelfth grades, generally reckoned to be a time of tension between adolescents and their parents.

So in 1930 Jack and Ruby began dating. His place was at Declo; she was a student in nearby—within eight miles or so—Albion. With a snappy Model A Ford, young Simplot grew well acquainted with all the picnic spots and places where courting couples felt secure. When asked where Jack proposed, Ruby responded that she was sure it was in his car.[5]

The wedding of John R. Simplot "white, of Burley, Idaho, age 21 years, 11 months, and 28 days," a "farmer," and Ruby Rosevear, "white, of Glenns Ferry, Idaho, age 20, 6 months, and 12 days," a "student," (she dropped out of school before the wedding) took place in Ontario, Oregon, on December 2, 1931, in the home of the presiding minister, the Reverend Samuel Allison of the Methodist Episcopal Church. The witnesses were Mrs. Allison and Mrs. Ralston. With the necessary documents filed at the courthouse in Vale, Oregon, the couple then began the honeymoon, probably in a Pontiac automobile by this time, eventually visiting Portland, Oregon, before returning to Declo to settle down in a primitive two-room farm house on Jack's rented place.[6] When they moved into town as prosperity came their way and after Jack's farm sale, the amenities of the Enyeart Hotel must have seemed almost luxurious as the farm pump and outhouse were replaced by its interior plumbing.

Ruby describes the accommodations and their time at the Enyeart in this manner:

> *On the first floor it had this two-room. . . we'll call it an apartment. And it did have an indoor toilet. So we did have that. But in order to have a shower or tub we had to go upstairs to where they* [admitted] *the other guests . . . . We were there a year or so. And then we moved right from there into Roosevelt, or Burton Avenue, I guess it was, in Burley. And that was a real nice step up. That was a nice house, and we were pleased with it. We lived there quite a few years. We lived there until we moved to Caldwell.*
>
> *He was still farming to some extent* [while living in Burley]. *But he also had to find a way to finish up this potato business and sell them. So it was an easy transition, that the potatoes had to go into a big storage cellar, and from there on it was to meet people and sell them out of state.*

Did Ruby have any role in the conduct of Jack's business?

> *Not much. When he first started with storing potatoes he also began to store potatoes in this long warehouse—other people's potatoes. And so therefore for just a little while I was the bookkeeper, a very short time because it soon grew beyond me. And those were the days when he would load a boxcar of potatoes, and in order to keep them from freezing, because it was fall, of course, he would go around with heaters and . . . I worried so much about Jack getting asphyxiated by working with those heaters in those [cars]. It was just a real worry to me.*[7]

As Simplot prospered, other moves occurred—from Burley to Caldwell, Idaho, and finally from Caldwell to Boise. But not yet. Two boys were born before the Simplots left Burley. And according to company information, somewhere between twenty-five and thirty farms were bought and sold in the 1930s.[8] Simplot's love affair with land has been life-long, but with a straight face he often remarks that he likes to acquire only the land that borders on his own.[9]

The year 1941 was pivotal in the ascending fortunes of J. R. Simplot. Approximately 1,000 employees worked at more than thirty potato and onion packing sheds with at least three sorting machines in each from which 10,000 boxcars were shipped annually. He paid five cents a bag for field run potatoes and received fifteen cents per bag for sorted ones, a profit margin of 200 percent, grossing the industrialist more than $500,000 a year, which netted out about $15,000.[10] The stern lessons of thrift and industry—save your money and work hard—learned from his father's precept and example and incorporated into his own internal gyroscope seemed to be paying off.[11] But the question remains whether agricultural practices of 1941 would continue to satisfy the expectations of this boundlessly ambitious Westerner.

Chapter Six Notes

1. JRS, 9-16-98, tape 1, side B.

2. JRS, 9-16-98, tape 2, side A.

3. JRS, 9-16-98, tape 2, side A.

4. Ruby Rosevear Shipp, subsequently RRS, 7-29-99, tape 1, side A.

5. RRS, 8-5-99, tape 1, side A.

6. RRS, 8-5-99, tape 1, side A.

7. RRS, 8-5-99, tape 1, side A.

8. Karen Simkins, "A Chronology of the J. R. Simplot Company" (J. R. Simplot Company, photocopied sixty-page document, 1993) 5. This vital resource lists in considerable detail activities going on in what year within the five principal divisions of the Corporation—Food; Minerals & Chemical; Agriculture; Diversified Products; and Corporate. The activities are listed as New ventures and new ideas; Acquisitions; New products and new processes; Expansion and changes to current businesses; and Closures and dispositions. It will be quoted from time to time to help indicate that the dynamism of its founder was objectively correlated by or to or within the Corporation.

9. As an example of the humor of understatement in folk speech, one can compare this comment with that of Ray Christensen (prominent Oregon Slope farmer and former champion wrestler, now deceased), who, upon being asked how he liked his new twelve-cylinder Lincoln Zephyr, replied that he liked it fine except that there always seemed to be another car ahead of him.

10. George Gilder, *The Spirit of Enterprise* (New York: Simon and Schuster, 1984) 30.

11. Although Jack's internal gyroscope was surely energized and set in motion by his father, in one interesting respect they differed. Jack's inner-directedness allowed more time for recreation than did his father's scheme. Thus the son could be found relaxing on the ski slopes and participating in hunting expeditions and fishing excursions beyond the necessity of providing for the family larder. Horseback riding, once a part of his work as a stockman-farmer, became a source of recreation, and he enjoyed golf.

Chapter Seven

The 1940s: War and growth

In the labor of engines and trades and the labor of the fields I find the developments, and find the eternal meanings.
Walt Whitman ("A Song for Occupations")

The new decade—the '40s—had dawned cloudy and grim in the Snake River Valley with the threat of rain and snow likely in the mountains. It all seemed an appropriate accompaniment to the war in Europe, which, except for early limited successes by the Finns, was not going well.

Pre-Christmas 1939 advertisements in the Caldwell, Idaho, *News Tribune* had featured 600 x16 tires for $6.75, 550 x17 for $6.10. If a customer wished to send a ten pound box of Idaho bakers to a friend anywhere in the United States, a local grocery would undertake the task for $1.23, including the potatoes and the costs of shipment. Nothing about the quality of the new year predicted what was to happen to Jack Simplot and his industry.

The new decade was just over a year old when a meeting in Chicago set in motion waves of energy that would transform the potato business. On January 23, 1941, representatives of a food manufacturing association—the Dehydrated Food Manufacturers of America—assembled to consider how that industry might participate in national defense. Colonel Paul P. Logan, Assistant Quartermaster General of the United States Army, attended this meeting as did John A. Sokol, founding president of Chicago's Sokol and Company. After Col. Logan outlined the Army's position with respect to dehydrated foods, he and Sokol began a search of the country for locations where dehydration plants might be established.

Sokol and Company had handled distribution of dehydrated vegetable products for a firm in Burbank, California, for nearly a decade. Sokol's company had also provided financial backing for the firm as necessary. Among the products dehydrated by the Burbank Corporation were onions, some of which were supplied by J. R. Simplot. Interestingly enough, it was indebtedness by the corporation to both Simplot and Sokol that brought about a meeting of the two in July of 1941 in Burbank, California.[1] It's a story Simplot enjoys telling:

> *This guy* [Burbank president Milton Grosz] *owed me $8,500, and I was down there tryin' to get it. And I ran into this guy* [Sokol] *he was sellin' his onions to, and I made a deal the same day I met him. Nice guy. And we wrote* [a contract] *on the back of an envelope we picked up there at that hotel.*[2]

According to one source, that contract reads as follows: "On or before October 1, 1940 [sic], Mr. J. R. Simplot agrees to commence shipping 300,000 pounds of onion powder at 21 cents a pound F. O. B. Idaho and 200,000 pounds of onion flakes at 31 cents a pound F.O.B. Idaho."[3]

Apparently, something like the following had happened. In an effort to collect the money owed him, Jack Simplot drove from Idaho to Burbank, California, a long day's drive, put up at a hotel, and the next morning appeared bright and early at the office of Milton Grosz, who was not in. Jack would wait. While he waited, another visitor arrived, also desiring to talk to the Burbank president about an unpaid bill. When noon came but Grosz did not, the two men agreed to have lunch at Jack's hotel, where the contract was worked out.

> *I never went back to see that guy* [Grosz] *till the next day, 'cause I went from there and drove down to see if I could find out what the hell he was doin' with his onions. And I followed a truckload of onions out there about six miles, and he turned into this prune orchard, and I went in and I got the name of the goddamn machine they were drying these onions with, and it was up north that he had his shop. And I drove up there the same day, and I bought a six-tunnel dryer from him. Because he built this damn thing, he knew all about it. And he helped me build the one in* [Caldwell]. *But in my contract with him* [Sokol] *he and I were gonna go 50/50 on this thing. And he sent*

> *out a guy from Chicago and made me put a lab in it and inside toilets. I wasn't figurin' on anything like that; y' know, that's expensive stuff. But I put 'em and said, "Send me some money,""and he never sent a penny 'til he got his first shipment of . . . onions. And I shipped 'em, and they were just what he wanted, and he sent me a check for seventy-five thousand bucks. And I had to send it back and say, 'Fella, you're just too late, because I had to get money to build this thing, and you didn't send me any." But he* [met] *all of his contracts. . . . The first year I ran the damn thing I made a half million bucks.*[4]

Some omissions need to be filled. Simplot had noted that the manufacturer's name on the prune dryer was the Knipchild Manufacturing Company, Santa Maria, California. He drove there and dealt for a six-tunnel dryer to be sent to Idaho, thinking he would probably set it up in the small town of Parma, to the west of Caldwell, Idaho. However, better arrangements were offered by the Caldwell Chamber of Commerce on a five-acre site two miles west of town immediately adjacent to the railroad branch line connecting Caldwell, Greenleaf, and Wilder. Jack himself outlined the plant, which consisted initially of two buildings, one on the eastern and the other on the western side of the site. The western building contained about 4,800 square feet and was utilized for packing and storage. The eastern building, slightly less than twice as large (8,000 square feet) held the drying tunnels.[5] To take charge of this new enterprise, Simplot organized the J. R. Simplot Dehydrating Company, which, as might reasonably be supposed, worked closely with the pre-existing Simplot Produce Company.[6]

By late August 1941, construction of the plant, which, it was hoped, would process two-and-a-half railroad cars of onions per day, began. Target date for completion was October 1, 1941, but that had to be postponed until October 8. Trial runs began, a bit of fine tuning was called for, and on October 9, the plant was running. And just in time, as circumstances proved, for on October 17, stimulated by his contacts with Sokol and the Burbank Corporation and supported by Sokol's connections with the Quartermaster Corps and Colonel Logan, Simplot met with Sokol and Logan to discuss the possibilities of dehydrating vegetables for the Army.[7]

Simplot's presentation must have been persuasive, and indeed his plant was beginning to amass staggering statistics. By the end of the onion season, he had processed 175,000 sacks of onions yielding more than a million pounds of dried onions. It is not surprising that the Chicago Quartermaster Depot of the U.S. Army on February 18, 1942, issued a contract to the Simplot Dehydrating Company, the first of many. Next, Simplot could turn his energies to the dehydration of potatoes, for which there were waiting government orders.[8]

Writing in the October 27, 1881, issue of the *Idaho Tri-Weekly Statesman*, a perspicacious journalist had anticipated the benefits of dehydrating potatoes and other vegetables and fruit, reducing them "to one-fourth of their original bulk" and lowering thereby "the cost of hauling the product[s] to markets."[9] Writing specifically about potatoes, the journalist observed:

> "A bushel of potatoes weighs sixty pounds, and by [evaporation] it can be condensed to thirteen pounds at an expense of about nine cents per bushel. At present it costs two cents per pound to haul a bushel of potatoes from Boise City to Hailey, a distance of 144 miles. This is $1.20 per bushel. But if you evaporate the water and condense your bushel of potatoes into thirteen pounds of bulk, your freight is but twenty-six cents or a clear savings of eighty-five cents upon your bushel of potatoes."[10]

In the late 1930s Simplot had chosen to do some experimenting with chemical fertilizers, purchasing a carload of fertilizer for his potatoes from the Pacific Guano Fertilizer Company of California. Although he did not know it at the time, his attempts to apply the material to a forty-acre field provided him with an experimental plot and a control, for the fertilizer applicator expended the carload long before the entire field could be treated. When the field was harvested, that portion receiving the fertilizer produced a magnificent yield of large tubers whereas the portion that was unfertilized produced few, and they were undersized. Ever the pragmatist, Jack Simplot was convinced and with characteristic passion attempted to get farmers and schools of agriculture to use, in the one instance, and recommend, in the other, fertilizer for potatoes. There was considerable reluctance to do so, but Jack knew what he knew, and his decision to go ahead on his own ultimately led to the formation of Simplot Soilbuilders, a not inconsequential segment of the Simplot organization.

Dr. William Webster Hall, third president of The College of Idaho often told the story of an aquaintance approaching him in Boise one afternoon with the information that "Jack Simplot bought a mountain today," stimulating Dr. Hall to ask Simplot the next time he saw the industrialist whether this report were true:

"No," Simplot snorted. "It's not true. I bought a range of mountains."[11] It was this mountain range that provided the phosphate for the Simplot Fertilizer Company, one of the largest fertilizer manufacturers on the continent.

People who know J. R. Simplot agree one of his strengths is an uncanny ability to select good people to work for him and to demonstrate the good sense to let them alone and not interfere as they went about those tasks. It must be a very great temptation indeed, especially for one with a wide-ranging intelligence, great curiosity, sound judgment, and large ambitions, to want to tell employees what to do and when to do it. With few exceptions, however, Simplot learned to refrain. With the dawn of a great day of company expansion here at the beginning of World War II, it is appropriate to identify some of the men who secured and later sustained that expansion.

Cliff Simons has been identified, as has Burdell Curtis, but he was not the only Curtis employed by Simplot. Two brothers also worked for the company, Blaine and Perry. Blaine ran the Unity packing shed, and Perry kept the books for the growing Caldwell complex. Leon Jones, hired in 1942 as a purchasing agent, was quickly elevated to production manager in charge of potato dehydration contracts. Jones, according to *Origins of the J. R. Simplot Company*, was destined "to become the preeminent figure in the company's food division for the next 28 years."[12]

Also hired in 1942 was Ray Dunlap, a chemist. A 1939 graduate of what was then the The College of Idaho, Dunlap is credited with solving the problems of satisfactorily freezing french fried potatoes. In 1943 Ralph Nyblad joined the company and utilized his first couple of years studying the potential for expanding wholesale and retail fertilizer markets. The result was "Simplot Soilbuilders." Right after World War II, a man was hired who made significant contributions to the enterprise Simplot was putting together, Grant Kilbourne, a pilot who, in Simplot's words, "could do anything."[13] In December 1945, Ray Kueneman, a 1937 graduate in food technology from the University of California, came into the organization as director of research and development.

The list of highly competent men chosen by Simplot continues with the procurement in 1946 of John Dahl, a 1938 business administration graduate of the University of Minnesota, Certified Public Accountant as of 1941. He was serving as an officer in the Quartermaster Corps when the name J. R. Simplot came to his attention He could hardly have dreamed that he would be the first to follow J. R. Simplot as company president in 1973.

Joe and Ben McCollum from the University of Arkansas went to work for Simplot in the middle forties, Joe McCollum having served as a food inspector in the Caldwell plant for the Quartermaster Corps, then returning to work for Simplot following his discharge from the army in 1946 after World War II. Ben was encouraged to come west in 1948, when he went to work for his brother in the Twin Falls Soilbuilder Unit and eventually became president of the Minerals and Chemical Division.

Paul Hansen chose to go with the J. R. Simplot Company in 1951. He grew up in Utah, was educated there (political science, marketing, agronomy at BYU), and came to Idaho to teach vocational agriculture. For Simplot he held a variety of jobs from fieldman to vice president.

Bob Whipkey joined the company in 1951 as a pilot, retiring as manager of real estate. Hugo Dalsoglio went to work for the company in 1952 and was on the payroll for forty-three years, advancing from the potato sorting line to a vice presidency.

Starr Farish was another who joined the company in 1952 as national sales manager. The next year the firm was joined by a chemical engineer named A. Dale Dunn. He might have been surprised had he looked into a crystal ball and seen that he would advance through the chairs from process engineer to plant manager at Pocatello to president of the company. He was succeeded in that capacity by Gordon Smith, who, in turn, was succeeded by Steve Beebe, who had been hired in 1970.

Other employees with extensive service records include Hugh Larkin, hired in 1953; John Basabe, in 1955, Bob Lothrop, 1959; Bill Daniels, 1959. These were loyal, productive, capable people, living testimonials to the creative mind that hired them or concurred in their being hired. They were expected to do their jobs and were allowed to do so.

The *Chronology of the J. R. Simplot Company* notes that "all expansion and growth of the world's largest potato dehydrating plant was accomplished without any government financing, not even a cost-plus contract" and affirms that "Simplot prices were the lowest of those supplying dehydrated potatoes to the Quartermaster." Simplot supplied something in the order of thirty-three million pounds of potatoes and five million pounds of onions between 1942 and 1945.[14]

The 1940s were years of expansion, military contracts vital in the first half of that decade with imaginative adjustments to peacetime taking up the slack in the second half. But it was not easy. One writer affirms that it was in the middle forties that Jack Simplot for the only time in his life was near breaking down.[15] A significant source of tension was the unceasing search for capital; another lay in his passion for ridding himself of the many—perhaps as high as fifty-two partnerships he had formed during the war years in order to take advantage of tax breaks they afforded:

Y'know, when I got my business goin', that's

> *all I could do was run my business. That was a big job for me because I wasn't any Houdini. And I had to make the decisions, and I kept the thing goin'. And we built, and built, and built! And I never took on another partner. I got my belly full of partners during the war! I said no more partnerships for me; I'll paddle my own canoe, and that's how I've kept the damn thing.*[16]

A brief comparison of John D. Rockefeller, Sr. and J. R. Simplot reveals interesting similarities in this matter of the difficulty of obtaining capital. Money that had been promised by Mr. Sokol—$50,000— for the construction of the plant at Caldwell was not forthcoming and Simplot had to borrow from an unidentified source. For both Simplot and Rockefeller there was never enough capital to do what they wanted to do. Rockefeller's biographer has this to say: "For all his populist mistrust of bankers, Rockefeller owed much of his incandescent rise to their assistance" and quotes the billionaire as saying, "The hardest problem all through my business career was to obtain enough capital to do all the business I wanted to do and could do, given the necessary amount of money."[17]

And time and time again Simplot had to marshal assets to provide collateral for loans, for he refused to stand still. His business was pulsating with life, and new prospects were constantly appearing, each with its price tag.

In 1943, for instance, the company expanded its farming and ranching segment in a significant way by acquiring three magnificent properties: Grand View

Farms (about 1,200 acres), Jamieson Farms (about the same size), and the Bruneau Sheep Company (one of the largest sheep outfits in the United States at around 30,000 head). This same year he built a feedlot in Caldwell and began feeding wastes from the potato processing operation—skins, sprouts, and eyes—to 2,000 hogs.

Then there was the problem of getting the dehydrated potatoes and onions safely to their overseas destinations. The answer was wooden containers, the production of which called for a box factory for their manufacture. Situated adjacent to the potato processor at the Caldwell plant, the factory soon employed twenty-two workers and turned out 20,000 board feet per day. In 1944 he organized the Caldwell Lumber Company and bought a sawmill at Horseshoe Bend, Idaho, which included a planing mill and presto log-shaping machinery to utilize the waste; it had a capacity for producing thirty-five tons per day.

To assure sufficient lumber for the box factory, in 1945 Simplot acquired an interest in Cal-Ida Lumber, which had a sawmill in Downieville, California, adding new equipment to the box factory which more than doubled its output. At the same time, that is, in 1945, he translated the hog-feeding program in Caldwell into a cattle-feeding operation by organizing Caldwell Feeders and building feedlots to accommodate 500-1,000 head of cattle.[18]

From the earliest of Simplot's ventures, he was aware of the economies of production, of the desirability of letting one activity feed into another, one process derive from another. This is not to suggest that it has been awareness only; it has been the capitalization upon the awareness to a remarkable degree that makes Simplot if not unique at least rare. Recall his entry into the world of finance by buying teachers' warrants, purchases secured by earlier profits from the rescue of bum lambs, all of which made possible the acquisition of a huge number of cheap hogs. When farming, he saw the wisdom of sorting and shipping his own potatoes, eliminating middlemen in the process. How appropriate to this entire matter was the generation of fertilizer . . . his own fertilizer, of course.

The utilization of cattle to consume waste products from potato processing is part of this awareness of production economies. When such wastes as peelings, sprouts, and culls were mixed with alfalfa, barley, and supplements in the early or experimental period of cattle feeding, the formula called for fifteen percent waste to eighty-five percent conventional feed. However, as the process was refined the percentage of waste material jumped to sixty-five percent, and the number of cattle on the feedlot could be increased from 4,500 to 150,000.

Another statistic is interesting: while it cost most feeders twenty-four cents to put a pound of meat on a steer, Simplot could do it for eighteen to twenty cents, thanks to the availability of low-cost wastes.[19] And the economy of production doesn't stop with feeding cattle; it includes the development of slaughter houses and the marketing of his own beef. Production economies, moreover, include the cow-calf operations on his many ranches through which feeder cattle are produced.

With respect to Simplot's refineries and manufacturing plants, careful attention is paid to recycling or re-using any by-product that can be so utilized, rather than wasting it. Thus water is carefully managed and recirculated so that it can be used again and again, gases are controlled with the same thrifty management, and any heat produced as a by-product of whatever chemical processes generate heat is viewed as a resource to be managed and utilized wherever possible. Such economies of production go far toward meeting the test of ecological and environmental morality.

There is another similarity to Rockefeller. The oil baron's biographer provides illustrative material by citing Rockefeller's plans to convert residual sulfuric acid, a by-product of the oil refining process, into fertilizer, and also the oil man's reaction to what seemed to be an eternal shortage of barrels by deciding to build his own cooperage. Suspicious of a plumber's bill, he instructed an associate to engage a plumber by the month and purchase their own plumbing needs. And of course Rockefeller's young refining business would do its own hauling.[20] Likewise with Simplot: if wooden crates can't be found in which to ship containers of dried potatoes, build your own box factory; if wood isn't available from which the crates can be shaped, buy your own sawmill.

Partnerships, borrowed capital, expansion, acquisition of a mountain range of phosphate deposits, repayment of loans: add to all this Dr. Hall's importuning for assistance with funding at the College of Idaho, pleading that led ultimately to funding for the first new building on the campus in several years, the stately and commodious Simplot Hall. It was no

Simplot family album

Richard Bonson
Jack's great-grandfather.

Simplot family album

Cornelius and Jane Nelson Haxby, J. R. Simplot's maternal grandparents.

Simplot family album

Elizabeth Nelson
Jack's great-grandmother.

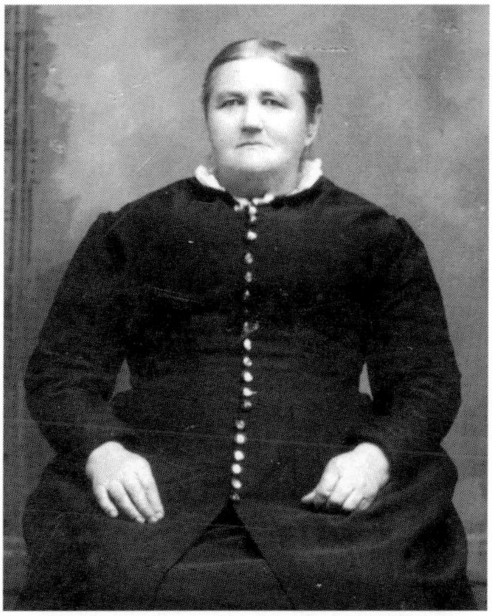

Simplot family album

Jack's maternal great-grandmother, Dorothy Bradley Haxby

Simplot family album

Susan Le Clere Simplot
Born 1811, Died 1876.

Simplot family album

Charles LeClere Simplot
Born 1838, Died 1900.

Simplot family album

Mary Bonson Simplot
Jack's paternal grandmother

Simplot family album

Charles Richard Simplot
Age 12.

Simplot family album

Dorothy Haxby Simplot
Age 12 or 13.

Simplot family album

J. R. Simplot's parents, Charles Richard and Dorothy Haxby Simplot, pose for their wedding photo, January, 4, 1904.

Simplot family album

Charles Richard Simplot, left front, hams it up for the camera with some Dubuque, Iowa, buddies.

Simplot family album

The Simplot family lived in this log cabin on their Idaho homestead while Dick was building a house. Jack is crouching by his father's knee.

Simplot family album

Dorothy Simplot poses in the doorway of their first Idaho cabin with children Myrtle, left, Jack and Margaret.

Burley, Idaho, Main and Idaho streets, 1912.

Simplot family album

Margaret, left rear, Myrtle, center and Jack Simplot beat the summer heat with a soak in an irrigation ditch near their home. The girl in the foreground is Vivian Hudson, who worked for the Simplots.

Simplot family album

Jack, left rear, poses with childhood friends, the "Baker Boys," of Burley, Idaho.

Simplot family album

The grade school class at Todd School, Santa Rosa, California. Jack, wearing bib overalls, is fourth from the left in the back row.

Simplot family album

The Simplot "ranch" in Santa Rosa, California, with Jack and younger brother Robert in the driveway.

Simplot family album

The Simplot children outside their Santa Rosa, California, home: Bob, left front, Margaret, Dorothy, Myrtle and Jack.

Simplot family album

Dick, left, and Jack gather eggs at the Santa Rosa chicken ranch for two unidentified customers.

Simplot family album

Left to right: Dorothy, Ethel, Bob, Jack and Bob, the family dog.

Simplot family album

Left to right: An unidentified toddler, Margaret, Jack and Dick Simplot, near Eugene, Oregon.

Simplot family album

Jack, left, and Dick Simplot with Jack's bum lambs, near Marsh Creek, Idaho.

Simplot family album

A little baseball after school? Jack, left, with his buddy Marshall Tollman. Marshall was one of fourteen children.

Simplot family album

Jack, top right, was only seventeen when he posed for this photo in 1926 as a member of Company “C” 162nd Infantry, Oregon National Guard.

Simplot family album

Jack with his big team.

Simplot family album

Jack, left, and Harley, Andy and Lindsay Maggart, pose with a pile of horseshoes during a visit to Yellowstone National Park.

Simplot family album

Jack's parents, Richard and Dorothy Simplot, in middle age.

Simplot family album

Jack and one of the Enyeart girls, daughter of the owner of the Enyeart Hotel in Declo, Idaho.

Simplot family album

Jack and Ruby Simplot, about 1930.

Simplot family album

The Simplot family. From left: Dorothy, Ruby, Dorothy, Dick, Jack, Bob and Margaret (kneeling).

wonder that Steve Richardson's query to Simplot in the J. R. Simplot Company History Project (CHP) elicited a passionate response. Simplot was asked why he moved from Caldwell to Boise in 1947:

> *Well I'll tell you why. I got more than I could handle. I was trying to run Caldwell and run Pocatello both . . . and I was going day and night and I couldn't sleep, and I was taking these sleeping pills. And that was the only habit I ever got into, but I had to buy those damn sleeping pills to get any rest. . . . Well, I got to see, hell, I can't do it. I just pooped out trying to run both of 'em . . . . So one day I wasn't feeling too good, and I'd never been sick a day in my life . . . . And I decided, by God, I can't handle her. I gotta get some help. And so I put* [Leon] *Jones in to run the potato operation, and he done me a hell of a job, and I moved to Boise. Then I hired another manager for Pocatello and got out from under that.*

However, before the Simplots left Caldwell in 1947, their family increased. Gay Corrine Simplot was born on February 1, 1945, the only daughter born to Jack and Ruby. The next year on October 11, 1946, their last child, Scott Robert Simplot, was born in Boise.

So Caldwell lost a powerful citizen, and a triumvirate emerged to take the potato portion of the food division to a height no one anticipated. Leon Jones, Ray Kueneman, and Ray Dunlap proved to be names memorable to the company. The young Minnesotan

John Dahl, whose fiscal astuteness was so essential to the Company's health, was hired in 1946. Who, way back in 1894, could have predicted that the Carey Act of that year, and who in 1902 would have thought that that year's Reclamation Act would have had such powerful consequences, helping win a war by providing nutritious food for armed forces and incidentally starting a young man on the road to becoming a billionaire? The humble potato truly deserves its celebration by writers.

Chapter Seven Notes

1. Information about the Chicago meeting, Sokol, and Logan is from the thirty-six page 1997 publication of the J. R. Simplot Company titled "Origins of the J. R. Simplot Company," pages 9-10. Compare this account with that of George Gilder, *The Spirit of Enterprise* (New York: Simon and Schuster, 1984) 30-31.

2. JRS 10-22-98, tape 1, side B.

3. George Gilder, *The Spirit of Enterprise* (New York: Simon and Schuster, 1984) 30-31. Gilder also asserts that Sokol agreed to put $50,000 into the Simplot dehydrator.

4. JRS 10-22-98, tape 1, side B.

5. JRS 10-22-98, tape 1, side B.

6. "Origins of the J. R. Simplot Company," 12.

7. "Origins of the J. R. Simplot Company," 13.

8. "Origins of the J. R. Simplot Company," 15.

9. Cited in James W. Davis, *Aristocrat in Burlap: A History of the Potato in Idaho* ([Boise, Idaho]: Idaho Potato Commission, 1992) 12.

10. In Davis, *Aristocrat*, 12.

11. *The Small College Talks Back: An Intimate Appraisal* (New York: Richard R. Smith, 1951) 196. A consideration of the rhetoric of Mr. Simplot's reply—"rhetoric" meaning the effective arrangement of his words—suggests that what he may actually have said was, "I bought a mountain range."

12. p. 17.

13. J. R. Simplot Company History Project, hereafter CHP, a series of audiotape recordings done by Steve Richardson of key figures in the Simplot organization, including Mr. Simplot, who said the following of Grant Kilbourne: "Grant Kilbourne flew me until I put him running the plant at Pocatello. And he was a pilot and secretary. He could take shorthand, and he could type, and he could write letters. He could do anything, Grant Kilbourne could, and I finally let him run the Pocatello operation, and he built a hell of a thing for me." December 13, 1995. All of the figures named here with their date of hiring were interviewed as part of this project.

14. Simkins, 6. "Origins of the J. R. Simplot Company" asserts that between

1942 and 1945 the company produced in excess of fifty million pounds of potatoes for the military (16). Whichever set of figures is accurate, it was a remarkable achievement, one that earned for the company two of the coveted Army-Navy "E" for Excellence awards.

15. Gilder, *Enterprise* , 36. If not the only time in his life, it was surely the first time Jack neared a breaking point. Three subsequent events proved to be of serious consequence, bending him, perhaps, but not breaking him.

16. JRS , 11-18-98, tape 2, side A. Exactly how many partnerships were formed is difficult if not impossible to say. Steve Jenning in "The Potato Billionaire" (*Northwest*, the *Oregonian's Sunday Magazine*, October 20, 1985) says that wartime corporate income tax designed to make profiteering difficult also made it difficult for Simplot to expand and that he sought to circumvent the problem by reorganizing his business into fifty-plus small partnerships with "friends, employees, [and] relatives" the beneficiaries; when peace came it was a major undertaking to restore himself to complete ownership. Jenning quotes Simplot as saying, "I had a helluva time [. . .] but it made a lot of them rich." (8) George Gilder, however, dealing expansively with the matter, writes as follows: "While working obsessively throughout the war and living in less luxury than most congressmen, J. R. Simplot managed to gain for himself a reputation as a profiteer and tax evader. To break the bottleneck of 90 percent rates, he created a sprawling complex of kited and cantilevered corporations, all punctiliously designed by Idaho's best legal talent. The company split into some ninety-five partnerships and scores of trusts held variously by Simplot, his family, his friends, his bankers, and his lawyers. It was all so far beyond his own expertise as an untutored trader and spud farmer that it made him nervous. But his lawyers assured him he was within the law, and the financial bottleneck was broken. Simplot was allowed to do his work supplying food for the troops." *The Spirit of Enterprise*, 34.

17. Chernow, Titan, 68.

18. Simkins, 6-7.

19. Charles J. V. Murphy, "Jack Simplot and His Private Conglomerate," *Fortune*, August 1968, 126.

20. Chernow, *Titan*, 79.

Chapter Eight

The postwar period: Redefining the market

Factories, mills, and all the processes of hundreds of different manufacturers grow thousands of words.
Walt Whitman, *An American Primer*, 1904
(published posthumously)

If Walt Whitman was delirious with words, Jack Simplot was intoxicated with deeds, with activity. Just as the Civil War had provided John D. Rockefeller "an opportunity to pile up riches,"[1] World War II challenged Simplot to show what he could do, and he was equitably recompensed for his efforts. It is not accurate, however, to call him a profiteer; there were no "cost plus" contracts, and income and excess profits taxes saw to it that profiteering did not materialize.

It is fair, however, to call attention to the role of the federal government in the opportunities it provided for the growth of the Simplot fortune. Perhaps that is the role—or at least one of the roles, along with the elimination of all forms of oppression—for which government exists.

The first instance of the use of federal money to provide opportunity lay in the various homestead and irrigation acts by which public lands became available for private ownership and productive once they were in private hands. The second instance is the military contracts for dehydrated vegetables ("fully a third of all their potatoes came from the . . . plants . . . of J. R. Simplot and his associates"[2]), the processing of which earned the Simplot firm the two Army-Navy Excellence awards, and much money.

Now, however, with the war over, peace declared, and demobilization occurring, what would happen to this man and his company? Two things happened immediately: sales of dehydrated potatoes declined to less than a fourth of their wartime level, and many of his partnerships materialized into living partners demanding cash for their holdings.[3] Among these was principal partner Charles Richard Simplot, who, fearing that his son was moving too fast and would go bankrupt, asked for an immediate cash settlement—$377,000 please!—although Dick placed the money in a trust fund for Jack and Ruby's children.[4] These two occurrences were fraught with gloom, and it appeared that Simplot might hurry down the path to oblivion along with other wartime entrepreneurs for whom there was no niche in the peacetime economy.

When company chemist Ray Dunlap approached Simplot with a request for a freezer, thinking aloud that it might be possible to combine the french frying and the quick freezing of potatoes, he was told that if you freeze a potato you get mush . . . but to go ahead and try it. According to Simplot:

> *I got him the box. He went to work and brought me in this pan of fries one day. He said, "These have been frozen." And they were good. I said, "That's a helluva thing."*[5]

In 1946 frozen french fried potatoes went into production; although the perfection of the product was a long way down the line, the launching of the company's flagship had been accomplished.[6] The evolution of the frozen french fry is an interesting story with pioneers (men like Dunlap and Kueneman), villains (chefs who controlled the market areas), and heroes (Simplot and Ray Kroc). Kueneman tells it this way:

> *I think we were on the market a little bit ahead of everybody else. That's my recollection. It didn't really make that much difference; we were looking for market wherever we could find it. All of our production was in retail pack, and of course the people in Maine had a freight advantage to areas like New York and Chicago over us here in Idaho. But we have the quality advantage.*
>
> *We tried desperately to get into the institutional market, to restaurants, the hotels, the mass feeders because you sell one housewife at a time package by package, but you sell an institutional user who buys his supplies for a certain period of time. And it wasn't until the*

late '40s or early '50s [that] *there was a national crop shortage on potatoes . . . . We thought, well, maybe with this shortage we can get into some of the market areas that we haven't been able to crack. Because we couldn't get them: the chef would spoil the product because he had a pyramid built up in his restaurant based on the number of people he had hired. The guys out there at the end peeling and stripping potatoes and so on were part of his domain . . . the pre-cooking and all the rest. With our product all they had to do was finish frying.*

I can remember buyers coming out from Chicago and New York and trying to run [a Simplot representative] down at one of the plants with a roll of bills about so big and say[ing], *"Hey, can't you let us have a couple of cars of potatoes?" By God, we're going to hold tough and we did. We got into Chicago and New York and Cleveland and some of the other cities, and once we had 'em, the general restaurant management could see the tremendous advantage because he didn't have to have all this damn staff of people to handle potatoes. In a minute he could have stuff on order out to the customer. That's what built the damn industry.* . .

It was tough. From '47 to '50 was tough, tough, tough. We had about ninety percent of the country's production on retail market, but . . . you were dealing with Safeway and a dozen other people who were in that [market]. *If we could get direct sales ourselves we could do a*

> *lot better. Of course the restaurant people wanted long strips.* [For] *most of the retail product, [length] wasn't stressed that much. You had to get it into a small packet, and it's easier to pack small potatoes, but on a restaurant plate if you take 100 grams of french fries and they're long, three to four inches, and drop them onto a plate . . . you get more plate coverage for* [fewer] *grams of finished product, and that was one of the sales things. This way they didn't have to deal with all the waste that came from their own kitchen preparation.*[7]

Why did the institutional market for frozen french fries finally take off?

> *The fact that we could get into the markets that we couldn't get into prior to that time. That we were just rebuffed by the chefs and so on. I spent some time with sales people and distributors myself calling on the trade, and that chef would kill ya every time. He'd just make it so that the quality wasn't there on the finished product and you had to find some way to get the management to look at what really could get done, and when fresh potatoes that were of high frying quality were not available, they still had customers asking for french fries. That broke the back and let us in.*[8]

Did the potato shortage at that time really play a significant role in the acceptance of frozen fries?

Yep, and the fact that our technology in storage [is] *fantastic. Forty or fifty years ago farmers would dig a pit, line it with straw, fill it with potatoes, mound it up and put the straw on and that was storage . . . all over the world and is today. But there was no temperature control, so consequently the earth which is a big source of temperature controlled what temperature the potatoes were exposed to in that pit. And it was low enough to where it kept the potato so that it was still a potato and not rot, but the starch would be converted to sugar, and you really couldn't fry those without 'em becoming as dark as my cane."*[9]

Ray Dunlap had indeed perfected the frozen french fry in his laboratory in response to the challenge delivered by his boss. It remained for Kueneman and his assistants to create the process for mass producing that product, losing none of the quality. The Dunlap-Kueneman Process in and of itself was sufficient to guarantee a unique immortality to the Simplot operation.

Kueneman said patenting the Dunlap process and its refinements was the next problem:

. . . I wrote several patents. And we had patent searches going back into the 1800s with a tremendous number of patents issued. Not only here but abroad. Eventually there was enough known about them that patenting wasn't going to give you the protection anyhow

because you could demonstrate prior knowledge in almost anything you wanted. The patents might not have worked . . . .

Was there a difference between the processes used by Simplot and the competition?

Yeah, in terms of process, and when they could do their very best, they had a nice product. But it didn't follow their patent. [At] *one of the IFT—Institute of Food Technology—meetings I met . . . some of the other guys and said, "Look, why don't you come out to Idaho, do a little fore-planning, and we'll give you a demonstration of what your patent describes, but we'll produce it with a different technology. Talk it over.*

I got Mr. Simplot introduced to Ray Kroc, and they became friends . . . . So we shipped them a whole bunch of finished product back to Chicago, and Ray Kroc and everybody said, "Well, it's better than what we do." I built a process line up in Heyburn to manufacture that in a direct line without all this fussing . . . and they took all we could make on that line. I had to continue expanding it, and I designed plant 2 and finally we just said, "Look, go get some other suppliers. You've got too much of our market, and we've seen what happens when a manufacturer gets to be a slave to a merchandising outfit.

Safeway was a classic example. They would contract for brewers and so on, and in some

> *year for no reason whatsoever except they felt like it, they would stop buying from that producer. We had one shot of that approach on canned corn. They had a contract for 60,000 cases of cream style corn, and we were just getting ready. We had started producing it, and the Safeway buyer came in and said, "Well, we don't want it," and Jones threw him out of the office. Within an hour I guarantee ya from coast to coast that was general knowledge: being thrown out of Simplot's, that Safeway buyer. But we had no trouble applying markup on it. . . .*

With the Safeway experience fresh in their minds, Simplot and his managers decided they never would dedicate all of their production to McDonald's, their largest customer. But Kueneman said McDonald's was very happy with the relationship:

> *. . . . They* [McDonald's] *were getting better quality than they had ever had, and they could start to expand their market. They could get into areas where it was just impossible to store potatoes, like the South.*[10]

This matter of storing potatoes takes on another dimension as George Gilder tells the story. McDonald's had bought raw potatoes from Simplot for some time, and although storage problems caused the hamburger operation to lose hundreds of thousands of dollars annually, the pre-Kroc management was not concerned. When Simplot suggested that the chain try his fries, prepared according to Simplot's and McDonald's patents, Kroc's predecessor was shocked that any one could think of doing such a thing. When Kroc became president, Simplot managed to get his potatoes tasted . . . and a friendship and business arrangement of benefit to both was sealed. Simplot has continued to supply the fries, and McDonald's has contributed about forty percent of the revenue and profit for the food division of the Idaho company.[11]

If Dunlap, Kueneman, and Jones (who probably did not physically throw the Safeway buyer out of his office, although he could have: Leon had been a second string All-American tackle in his football playing days at Utah) comprise the first triumvirate of the food division, John Dahl played an extremely significant solo role in shaping the fiscal management of the company. That he came to be employed by Jack Simplot gives further evidence of Simplot's ability to choose good people, to permit them to do their good work, and to reward them commensurately.

A CPA and Senior Accountant with Ernst and Ernst, Dahl was drafted in 1942, completed basic training, and was admitted to Officers Candidate School. Assigned eventually as a financial analyst to the Quartermaster Corps in New York City, Lieutenant Dahl began work analyzing financial statements of companies with government contracts, mainly in the food industry. Reassigned to San Francisco to head up the financial analysis section of the contract re-negotiation office of the West Coast division of the Quartermaster Corps, dealing principally with Western food processors, Dahl was assigned to undertake the analysis of the J. R. Simplot Dehydrating Company. It was inevitable that they should meet. The Company History Project records Dahl's memories of the early days:

> *I was at that time a second lieutenant . . . and Mr. Simplot's . . . company was one that . . . we were re-negotiating for excessive profits in contracting with the government. And I handled the financial analysis . . . and continued handling it . . . so I saw him, and he came down . . . to San Francisco a number of times . . . and I came up here to Idaho . . . in maybe late 1944-45 to his original plant . . . in Caldwell and met his people and inspected his plant layout . . . and got better acquainted with Jack at that time. So I was in the Quartermaster Corps in San Francisco . . . all through 1945 . . . . By the end of 1945 the war was over, and Jack was looking for other things to do because his dehydration contracts he presumed were going to be terminated. At that time he asked if I'd be interested in coming up to Idaho and working for him in the financial end of his business. . . .*[12]

Although Dahl had the opportunity to return to Minneapolis and work for Ernst and Ernst again as senior accountant, he and his wife found their way to Caldwell because, as he put it,

> *This looked like an interesting area around*

here, and Jack looked like an interesting guy to work for, and to work with, so I . . . became . . . the treasurer and the controller of whatever companies he had.[13]

So all of the economy work and the setting up of accounting systems and handling the finances in all these companies fell into my hands because up until that time . . . he had a bunch of bookkeepers that were handling the accounting on a local basis and nothing fancy, and he had . . . a tax accountant in Salt Lake City that was doing his tax work. So after I came with the company I took over all of that work, and that's how I started with the Simplot Company and got very familiar with all of the company operations and all the people that were here . . . .[14]

During and after the war, one heard the expression "excess profits tax" over and over again without really understanding what the fuss was all about. According to Dahl, it wasn't really a tax but rather "the recovery from government contractors of any . . . profits that would have been generated by any company in excess of a certain base percentage," with unusual or extraordinary expenses taken into account, with those that did not pertain to the processing of potatoes, as an example, disallowed. When the overall profit was calculated, any in excess of the profit level serving as a benchmark for the government was claimed by the government. At that point the contractor or his attorneys met with government negotiators so that agreement could be reached as to how much of the excessive profits should be returned.[15]

Did the Simplot Company stand out among the companies Dahl was dealing with as Quartermaster?

> *They were one of the companies processing food, but they were the major processor of dehydrated potatoes and onions. There were other small dehydrators on the West Coast but none with the capacity that Simplot Company had. But the Simplot Company really stood out. They were the number one processor, number one to deal with, very cooperative, and if the Quartermaster Corps needed . . . huge quantities of potatoes, well, the Simplot Company was always able to come up with it.*[16]

John Dahl provides further insights into the dynamics of the early Simplot organization. Dahl said when he went to work for Simplot after the war:

> *. . .the only office they had—you might say general office—was in Caldwell, and when I got there there were only three of us that would be considered the main company office, and I'm not counting the food division personnel; that was a separate unit . . . but there was Mr. Simplot and myself and . . . Grant Kilbourne. . . . The three of us made up that office in Caldwell, and we all lived in Caldwell for a year or so, and then we moved to Boise. . . . The start of the office was the three of us.*[17]

Chronologically, this arrangement might be called

the second triumvirate, although with respect to hierarchy, any group with Simplot as a member would be the alpha or true leadership group, "first," in the sense of being the overseer of all the operations. So this was headquarters, and Dahl was faced with the daunting task, as interviewer Richardson put it, of getting all the operations, all the partnerships, all the companies, even the tax accounting, under one rubric.

Even though each division of each company had its own sales staff, purchasing department, and accounting department, the books were generally in good shape, Dahl found. It was of concern, however, that headquarters was not getting financial statements, since the accounting system was mostly general ledger accounting: cash receipts, cash disbursements, and bank balances, and the like. Dahl believed that Jack never had a financial statement until the renegotiation of contracts in San Francisco required such a submission. Getting all of these more or less discrete operations into a unitary system of fiscal management and accounting meant that Dahl and Simplot traveled extensively, particularly among the three centers of activity: Caldwell, Burley, and Pocatello. Dahl estimated that from sixty to seventy percent of his time was spent away from home. And interestingly enough, unlike subsequent practices, those trips were undertaken by automobile.[18]

According to Dahl:

> *Jack's the type of guy that wants to operate by himself, and he didn't want any partners in effect telling him what to do. He wanted to*

> *make up his own mind.*[19]
>
> *The J. R. Simplot Dehydrating Company, as I remember, was incorporated in 1946 or 1947, and the name of the company at that time was changed to J. R. Simplot Company. In 1955—and this is strictly from recollection—we set up a company called the Simplot Investment Company, which we wanted to have as kind of a holding company for all of the other outside companies, and by merger most of them came into Simplot Investment Company. For instance, the J. R. Simplot Company was merged into Simplot Investment Company, and the produce company in Burley was merged in, also the Cal-Ida Lumber Company in California. And at that time the company name was changed to J. R. Simplot Company, and Simplot Investment Company became another company. But the J. R. Simplot Company became really the holding company overall.*[20]

If all that is a bit complex, another descriptive word helps characterize the condition of the Simplot operation and that is the word "surprising." The Simplot Company was a surprisingly complicated organism. It also is surprising how much the company relied on borrowed money. Again, there are remarkable similarities with the modus operandi of John D. Rockefeller, Sr., who publicly denied ever borrowing but privately—and inescapably—relied heavily upon bankers in the early stages of his career, from about 1863 to 1873.[21]

Dahl remembered:

We borrowed every nickel we could get our hands on and just hoped that we could generate enough cash to pay 'em back, and fortunately we did.[22]

Financing was a difficult thing. The company could not throw off profits and depreciation fast enough to keep up with the expansion that was needed at any of the companies, so we had to go to the banks, and that's what I dealt with principally . . . bank financing, or let's say insurance company financing . . . . Many years ago we started out with the Prudential Insurance Company for term financing. We later got in with Hancock Insurance Company . . . .

To begin with Jack and I went to the banks, and then sometimes we'd bring in managers of the divisions. For instance, Leon Jones was president of the Food Division and the manager. He'd join us. If we were talking about facilities in Pocatello, the fertilizer division, then we'd take Grant Kilbourne . . . .

I think every year we tried to borrow more money, because Jack wanted to expand all the time, and the managers . . . in the food division and fertilizer . . . wanted to expand all the time. There were lots of different types of financing that we undertook. Some of it was on a three or five year basis to pay back over that period of time; some of it was under a lease arrangement. Whatever way we could get money, that's the way we went. Sometimes we dealt directly with the banks; we finally ended up with the Continental Illinois Bank and Trust Company in Chicago, and we did a lot of banking with them. Over the years they did us a great job . . . but the bankers were tough. They wanted their money on time . . . and sometimes we had to really negotiate to get the loans extended. It was a trying time.[23]

One of the beneficial consequences of this perpetual cycle of borrowing may have been unanticipated. To establish a good credit rating among money lenders, two conditions are necessary. In the first place, credit must be used. It is one of the ironies of financial life that the individual or firm that always pays cash establishes no reputation as a good risk. And in the second instance, loans must be paid promptly or renegotiated in a timely manner. These two conditions are well known as foundation stones of creditor-borrower relationships. At no time did the Simplot organization jeopardize this relationship, and the good credit rating that resulted was an anticipated consequence. Charles Richard Simplot had wound up his son's gyroscope better than he knew. But there was an unanticipated benefit as revealed by dialog between historian Richardson and former executive Dahl.

Steve Richardson was curious about the budgeting process and asked Dahl how decisions were made and priorities established for the various divisions and the corporate office:

. . .Early on the banks insisted that we consolidate all of our financial statements. I think we had twenty or twenty-five companies that were all, you might say, in a different type of business, and with the staff I had in Boise, we consolidated all those financial statements. We didn't have any computers . . . [so] *we just put them on spread sheets and made the inter-company eliminations and so on because the banks wanted to see what the total profitability of the combined companies would be, not just segments of the company, but we had a pretty good idea of where the money was needed. For instance if the food division wanted to expand . . . we'd put together financial statements to project how much money we would need to borrow to double the capacity of the food division or likewise in Pocatello to upgrade the fertilizer facilities. But generally the money was allocated out where Mr. Simplot and the plant managers could see where the greatest improvement could be made. . . . Some years the potato business would be very good, and we needed to expand the potato* [processing] *lines.* [For example] *we had to expand our facilities in the food processing plants to handle the ever-increasing demand that McDonald's put on us. So these were generally the triggers as to where the money would go, and we tried to borrow money to fit into* [those needs]. *Later on we got each company to submit its capital expenditure requirements, and we'd go through that, Mr. Simplot, myself, and the company managers*

and determine how much each division would have because we were limited in the amount of money we could borrow. So it was really a bare bones operation. None of them could have as much money as they wanted. Some years we wouldn't spend any money for new trucks or things like that. We had to make do with what they had.[24]

The unanticipated benefit referred to earlier was the synoptic view of the operations Jack Simplot had put together. And because there was now a unified vision of the establishment with an overall view of things, strategic planning became possible, although that term would not have been employed back in 1955. Jack's general awareness of the needs, prospects, and triumphs of his company was always clear, and his mind was of such a quality as to be constantly ranging ahead and seeing beyond what is given most men. It is not stretching the truth to say that this quality is a kind of genius. However, even genius profits from discipline, and the discipline provided by this unified vision worked well for the company. No longer would there be the costly error of competition among different divisions of the company as had occurred when, for instance, the fresh produce unit found itself competing against processing plants for raw potatoes.[25]

A quick look at *A Chronology of the J. R. Simplot Company* gives some hint as to just how busy Jack Simplot was, realizing, of course, that in an enterprise of the magnitude of the Simplot company, the owner could not be everywhere and do everything. We know, too, that Jack chose his executives well and let them perform pretty much on their own hook, with a minimum of interference from above. Nevertheless, because it was *his* company and the ultimate responsibility and power lay with him, one can conclude that Jack Simplot was totally occupied if not consumed by his obligations to the company he had labored to put together. He viewed his company as part of himself.[26]

In 1955 twenty activities occurred, classified as six "New Ventures," twelve "Expansions," and two "Acquisitions"; five activities that seemed not to belong to established categories were included simply as "Notes."[27] The new ventures included the development of a fluorospar deposit at Myers Cove near Challis, Idaho; the formation of Simplot-Devoe Lumber Company, the construction of a sawmill at Chiloquin, Oregon, near Klamath Falls, and buying and cutting timber on Indian land under contractual arrangements with Indian agencies and the federal government; emphasizing products of the fertilizer division through an extensive advertising campaign on three Idaho TV stations while intensifying advertising in the print media; purchasing silica mine leases and a processing plant near Overton, Nevada, and forming Simplot Silica Products, Inc. to sell sand primarily to foundaries, to makers of glass containers, and to manufacture sodium silicate; and the operation of two dredges, one near Warren and the other on Baumhoff-Marshall ground near Sunbeam both in Idaho.

Acquisitions in 1955 consisted of the purchase of outstanding shares of Portable Lumber Company and the purchase of Three Creek Ranch (doing business as Diamond A Ranch) near Jarbidge, Nevada, as a cow-calf operation.

Although in 1955 there was no activity in the New Products component of the *Chronology*, Expansion was lively. Operations at the expanded Pocatello fertilizer plant resumed; Simplot Soilbuilders expanded through the opening of a new unit at Buhl, Idaho; Caldwell Lumber Company added a new 1,200-foot tramway to carry sawdust to a stockpile; the Food Division added a new fryer, an additional blancher, and a new conveyer at the Caldwell plant so that a retail and an institutional french fry line could operate simultaneously. At the same time the Caldwell processing plant started construction of a new potato warehouse featuring an underground flume that would float potatoes to processing lines. Also at Caldwell, the feedlot operation added a new—Williamson—feed mill for preparing livestock feed.

At Aberdeen, Idaho, a new potato storage cellar was built while the old warehouse was re-done and completely modernized. In Bakersfield, California, the firm opened a branch office for shipping potatoes. For purposes of distributing Simplot fertilizers in Utah, Simplot set up O. E. Muir and Company as exclusive agents. A new warehouse was added to the Burley potato processing plant, while at Aberdeen an anhydrous ammonia unloading station, complete with railroad spur, offices, shop, and warehouse was constructed. At Greeley, Colorado, Simplot Soilbuilders added offices and an experimental ammoniator, with a new storage building constructed at Klamath Falls,

Oregon. The Caldwell Simplot Soilbuilders component introduced two-way radio communications while the corresponding units at Blackfoot and Idaho Falls added new facilities.

The following will give an indication of the vitality of Simplot's operation and the demands on his time and energy as "Notes" begins with the following magisterial statement:

"All food processing units were placed under Division headquarters supervision at [the] Caldwell plant, and all marketing was handled by Sales Department, Caldwell—twenty products at this time, including frozen french fries, frozen potato patties, frozen diced potatoes, onion flakes, onion powder; canned and frozen corn, fruit and other vegetables, including 'minute' potatoes which were produced for General Foods Corp."

This statement is followed by the brief observation that on "June 26, 1955, J. R. Simplot Co. was incorporated [the incorporation was comprised of 28 companies and corporations]." The third note entry says that the firm "Produced a 27-minute film entitled *Harvest Hands* giving a tour of all company operations." Finally we see that Cal-Ida [a Simplot company] employees formed a credit union in Auburn, California, and that the credit union for Simplot employees in Pocatello opened on December 31.

From 1955 through 1959, twenty-six discrete transactions, activities, or proceedings of one kind or another were conducted, initiated, or concluded, to say nothing of loans paid or negotiated or re-negotiated.[28]

The 1950s was a time of reorganization and stabilization for John Richard Simplot and his company. He had proven his success wasn't just a war years' anomaly. As the new decade dawned, he was ready to expand both his business and personal horizons.

Chapter Eight Notes

1. Chernow, *Titan*, 68.

2. Gilder, *Enterprise* , 34.

3. Gilder, *Enterprise*, 35.

4. ibid.

5. "Origins of the J. R. Simplot Company" (Boise, Idaho: J. R. Simplot Company, 1997) 26.

6. Origins, 26.

7. CHP. October 3, 1995.

8. CHP. October 3. 1995.

9. CHP. October 3, 1995.

10. CHP. October 3, 1995.

11. *Enterprise*, 39.

12. CHP. August 17, 1995.

13. CHP. August 17, 1995.

14 . CHP. August 17, 1995.

15. CHP. August 17, 1995.

16. CHP. August 17, 1995.

17. CHP. August 17, 1995.

18. CHP. August 17, 1995.

19. CHP. August 17, 1995.

20. CHP. August 17, 1995. A less rococo statement of the compression appears in Simkins, *Chronology*: "June 26, 1955, J. R. Simplot Co. [underlining as in original] was incorporated (the corporation was comprised of 28 companies and corporations"). 15

21. Chernow, *Titan*, 104. Chernow quotes Rockefeller here: "One can hardly recognize how difficult it was to get capital for active business enterprises at that time" and then continues in his own voice to say that if Rockefeller ever groveled, he did so in his constant appeals to bankers, absorbing all the money available from Cleveland resources and having to turn to the greater supply available in New York.

22. CHP. August 17, 1995.

23. CHP. August 17, 1995.

24. CHP. August 17, 1995.

25. This insight comes from the Company publication "Origins of the J. R. Simplot Company" (1997), which goes on to say, "This intracompany competition eroded the profitability of the division. By the mid-1950s, the arrangement became unworkable, and the process of reorganizing the produce division and shutting nearly half of its produce sheds [began]." (30) A similar problem in the fertilizer component is discussed by Ben McCollum in the Company History Project (August 21, 1995), where there was "a little bit of conflict between the wholesale people and the Soilbuilders wherever they operated."

26. In commenting on the advisability of his firm being placed in public ownership and put on "the big board," Simplot is quoted by Charles J. V. Murphy in "Jack Simplot and His Private Conglomerate," *Fortune* [August 1968] 172: "Givin' up what I've built would be the same as givin' up part of myself."

27. This and the ensuing information is from Karen Simkins's chronological summary of the activities of the company, beginning with Jack's birth in 1909 and carrying through 1993. Titled simply "A Chronology of the J. R. Simplot Company" and published by the company in August of 1993, this volume will prove essential to anyone writing a history of the company and is, of course, extremely helpful to scholars whose primary interest is the biography of Jack Simplot. It is often difficult to separate the man from his company, for in a very real sense the latter is the objectification and alter ego of the former. Information for 1955 will be found on pages 15 and 16.

28. The *Chronology* faithfully itemizes these (17-18), and their importance for the biographer lies in their quantity, range, and scale, from the construction of potato storage sheds, opening mines, and starting new potato processing lines through phasing out sheep operations to the purchase of 14,300 acres in two ranches and the sale of the Jamieson farm. When the pragmatic Simplot became convinced that an activity or property was unprofitable, he got rid of it; by the same token, he was ever alert to new prospects and enterprises with promise. Indeed, he was a busy man.

Chapter Nine

The 1960s: Expansion

Nineteen sixty launched a decade (1960-69) of Simplot activities requiring eight pages of the Simkins *Chronology* (pp. 19-27). Included were the opening of the Heyburn, Idaho, frozen potato processing plant; the purchase of the complete fertilizer plant facilities of the Anaconda Company of Anaconda, Montana, and dismantling and shipping to Pocatello by rail and truck its ammonium phosphate plant; the leasing of ore mining operations at Conda Mine near Soda Springs, Idaho, along with a village for housing employees; starting production at a third Cal-Ida sawmill at Comptonville, California, (the three prepared and shipped about sixty million board feet per year). Finally, the company became partners with Potato Service Incorporated in building a processing plant at Presque Isle, Maine, to service primarily the Eastern United States. And these were only a few of the activities . . . for 1960!

In 1961 the Pocatello fertilizer plant was expanded;

its triple superphosphate capacity was enlarged by the addition of three Raymond grinding mills for reducing rock phosphate, by creating greater boiler capacity, by installing a plant-wide water-reclaiming system. With the addition of the necessary technology, the plant could now produce three types of ammonium phosphate, bringing the total annual production of phosphate fertilizer to about 360,000 tons a year. In eastern Idaho, 2,000 acres of productive land known as the Howe Farms were purchased. Then, to maintain a competitive edge, the firm began building a potato processing plant near Carberry, Canada, in the province of Manitoba, along with a cattle feedlot to recycle certain by-products of the processing of potatoes.[1]

The very next year the subsidiary "Simplot of Canada" opened its two-and-a-half-million dollar potato processing plant there for the production of dehydrated and frozen potato products for the Canadian market in affiliation with the Carnation Foods Company, Limited. Produced at this former air base, where three abandoned hangers had been joined to create the new facility, were frozen french fries, frozen Potato Gems, dehydrofrozen potatoes, and Instant Mashed Potato Granules. Not to neglect domestic opportunities, the company created at the Heyburn, Idaho, plant a production line for a pre-gelatinized potato starch for use in instant puddings and opened a new freezer warehouse while adding an automotive shop.[2]

In 1963 there were some thirteen separate positive

activities . . . and one costly fire . . . as varied as the opening of six new Simplot Soilbuilders units (at Bruce, Royal City, and Toppenish, Washington; Tulelake, California; Bayard, Nebraska; and American Falls, Idaho); the acquiring of a lease of phosphate-bearing federal land in southeastern Idaho and western Wyoming (the noteworthy Smoky Canyon site mentioned in the foreword); the leasing of 33,000 acres known as the Grouse Creek Ranch at Twin Peaks, Utah; the purchase of another silica operation adjacent to the Overton, Nevada, site; and the entering into a contract with Texas Gulf to supply sulfur to the Pocatello plant. The one costly fire destroyed the potato warehouse at Nyssa, Oregon, consuming the stored potatoes, supplies, and equipment.[3]

In 1965, there were some fourteen activities, including the naming of Leon Jones as the first president of the Food Division, Grant Kilbourne the first president of the Minerals and Chemicals Division, and George Duff president of the Lumber Division; launching construction of a thirty million dollar fertilizer plant at Brandon, Manitoba, Canada; and filing a multi-million dollar lawsuit against the Texas Gulf Sulfur Company, which immediately filed a countersuit. Not to be overlooked was the purchase of an additional 1,500 acres at Howe Farms.[4]

In 1966, The College of Idaho celebrated its diamond jubilee, and through a combination of good fortune and hard work, Nelson Rockefeller was featured as principal speaker at several of the events. Of course he would meet Jack Simplot in the week of these celebrations, and that meeting was the beginning of an interesting connection. Jack tells of his meeting this grandson of John D. Rockefeller, Sr., this way:

> *I went down one time with Rockefeller to his farm in Venezuela . . . . Ya, Nelson. Spent a week with him and his wife. He had an attorney with him, can't remember the attorney's name, but he flew me down out of Baltimore. He came out here to make a talk at our college, and I got acquainted with him, and I took him out and showed him my farms and my potato operations. It was in the fall of the year, and I had trucks lined up and potatoes coming in . . . and it impressed him, I guess. And he said, "Jack, I got a piece of land in Venezuela, and my brother and I financed the bulldozers . . . and they built this dam across twenty-one miles of it, and the dam's about twenty-five foot high, maybe thirty. They bulldozed it, all they took was two bulldozers down there, and they flew the gasoline in to keep 'em running, and they built this dike, and they shut the water off in the rainy season, and it backs up twenty-five, thirty miles. And as the summer comes . . . the grass grows where the water was." He told me they had 70,000 head of cows on it. I didn't see 'em when I was down there, but I saw a herd or two of 'em. He said, "It's been ten years, and I just can't get anything to town."*
>
> *Well, it didn't take me long . . . hell, the whole country was eating his cattle, that's all. And I got into the same deal down in Columbia*

> *where I planted, oh, several thousand coconut trees. I got some pictures somewhere of this coconut orchard I had . . . awesome. And I fertilized it, took fertilizer down there, and then I built a big place to put my coconuts, but I never got a coconut to town. Never sold a coconut! Everybody fifty miles around* [was] *livin' off 'em.. You can't shoot 'em. You come out there at night and you can hear 'em. But, hell, they'd steal every coconut soon as it got big enough to eat . . . . I had 65,000 hectares and eleven sawmills and four big plywood plants in Columbia . . . .* [When] *they started kidnapping* [employees] *and holding them for ransom, we just walked off and left $30 million worth of equipment and said, "Take it!" Helluva note—eleven sawmills, and I had a helluva thing going, but our coconut plantation went with it.*[5]

More details could be summoned from the *Chronology*, to secure the point that J. R. Simplot and his company were on top of things in the '60s, busy and occupied from "kin-to-cain't," that is, from early in the morning when you can just begin to see, to nightfall when you can't. However, a clear insight into the man and a concise summary of company activities—the two are virtually inseparable—comes from Pocatello's *Idaho State Journal* of August 14, 1968, in a feature story headed "Work Key Word in Simplot Story."

Identified in the feature as the wealthiest man in Idaho, Jack says he just went to work, and that's the story of his empire . . . which includes agriculture and livestock, chemicals, timber, and minerals in thirty-seven states and foreign countries. In addition to his phosphate resources on the Fort Hall Indian Reservation—"the biggest phosphate deposit west of Florida"—Simplot's mineral holdings include silica, clay, lead, zinc, barium, uranium, coal, copper, gypsum, and gold. He is quoted as saying, "I don't owe enough. If I could owe more, I could build more plants." As to his worth, the story speculates it is somewhere between $200 million and $500 million, although Simplot doesn't say whether either amount is close to accurate. And finally Simplot says he doesn't want to sell stock: "I just never liked to work for the other guy. I make the decisons and I enjoy makin' 'em." [6]

Although an issue of *Fortune* magazine that appeared in May 1969 omitted him from the list of sixty-six Americans whose personal wealth exceeded $150 million, by July the publication had identified Simplot as the wealthiest man in Idaho with an estimated fortune of $200 million. The earlier omission resulted from faulty estimates by Boise bankers, who had put his fortune at less than $100 million.[7] It is instructive to return to the *Chronology* for an examination of activities of the firm to see whether it would appear to the unpracticed eye that the company was thriving.

In 1967 J. R. Simplot and Ray Kroc agreed with a handshake to the use of Simplot french fries—called MacFries—at McDonald's. The plant at Brandon was brought completely on line, its storage facilities finished, and its capacity was established as 350,000 tons of fertilizer per year. A potato processing plant at Taber, Alberta, Canada, in affiliation with Carnation Foods Company, Ltd., began producing instant potato granules. The company won its judgment against Texas Gulf for more than $9 million; Texas Gulf filed an appeal. The fertilizer plant at Pocatello was expanded to the tune of $20 million, enhancing the production of sulfuric acid, anhydrous amonia, ammonium sulfate, ammonium phosphate, and phosophoric acid. The sell-off of the Ruby Company Farms in Minidoka and Blaine counties began. And that is only six of the eleven separate activities for the year. The next year there were a dozen activities, with the purchase of the heretofore leased Grouse Creek Ranch of Utah particularly notable.

In 1969, purchases, expansions, and sales dominated the eleven principal activities: the Burley potato plant capacity was increased through a $500,000 expansion program; Simplot Aviation took over Idaho Beechcraft; a second potato plant at Caldwell was begun, costing $10 million and increasing production by 70 percent; the lumber holdings were sold, except for an involvement in the mill at Auburn, California. And finally this: "Courts upheld a previous decision favoring the company in a lawsuit against Texas Gulf in the amount of $6 million."[8]

The company seemed to be prospering with J. R.'s energy and enthusiasm undiminished. If the estimate of Simplot's worth at $500 million was close to accurate, he was halfway to billionaire status.

Chapter Nine Notes

1. 20.
2. ibid.
3. 21.
4. 23.
5. JRS 9-16-98, tape 1, side A.
6. Allen M. Bailey.
7. *Idaho Statesman*, July 28, 1969.
8. 25-27.

Chapter Ten

The Simplot family

His own parents, he that had father'd him and she that had conceiv'd him in her womb and birth'd him,
They give this child more of themselves than that. . .
"There Was a Child Went Forth," Whitman

To say that Jack's parents, Dick and Dorothy Simplot, were cut from the traditional pattern of Victorian parental cloth is probably accurate. One can almost employ Walt Whitman's evocation of his own parents to describe them:

The mother at home quietly placing the dishes on the supper table / The mother with mild words, clean her cap and gown, a wholesome odor falling off her person as she walks by / The father, strong, self-sufficient, manly, mean, anger'd, unjust / The blow, the quick loud word, the tight bargain, the crafty lure . .

("There Was a Child Went Forth,"
from *Leaves of Grass)*

Although, Dick Simplot was not a Yankee, he nevertheless shared certain traits with Walter Whitman, Senior, and the tight bargain and crafty lure ("mind the main chance") are appropriately used to characterize Jack's father. Of his father, Jack said, "He died at ninety-one. I [have] to say the guy was a tough, hard-boiled cookie. I mean he ruled the roost. But he taught me . . . everything I know."[1]

In the primitive time before pop psychologists when we had no recourse to books and courses of instruction in parenting (one wonders whether there will be publications on brothering, sistering, cousining . . . the list of family relationships could be extended almost infinitely), one absorbed an understanding of how to be a mother or father by the precepts and examples of one's parents. That understanding was enhanced by a portion of whatever Mother Nature supplied by way of instinct and intelligence. The Victorian model is too well known to require comment, and in any case Dick and Dorothy Simplot are conveniently at hand for that purpose.

On March 7, 1934, Richard Rosevear Simplot was born in Burley, Idaho. On September 4, 1935, Don John Simplot was born in the same town. Dick and Don, only a year and a half apart, were often linked by observers as if they were twins and similar in all respects. Each lad was distinctive, but one of the major differences was the fact that at age five Dick developed diabetes. His mother says, "Dick was five years old, and he became so listless . . . . I went to Salt Lake [City] and put him in the hospital . . . . I would go down and stay and take lessons on how to feed him."[2]

Younger than Dick by a year and a half, Don John Simplot was born in 1935 when the family lived in Burley, having moved from nearby Declo. Like Dick, he had problems in school. After the first grade in Burley, he found school in Caldwell, the new family home, difficult, and the first grade was repeated. Then the Simplots moved to Boise, where the family troubles with reading and spelling caused him to be held back again.

When Dick and Don encountered problems with school in Caldwell, the responsibility for their remediation lay with Ruby. In the Victorian model, children were the responsibility of the mother and the nanny; father's job was to earn the living. With this family the arrangement was appropriate, because Ruby was familiar with theories of educational development, at least those that were current when she was in college. She had, after all, planned to become an elementary teacher. And Jack was busy enough for two men. However, the boys presented difficulties beyond her capability.

Dick and Don's learning problems seemed to involve word recognition and orthography, primarily, and a general insouciance regarding the whole idea of school. In addition to academic problems and an indifference to school there was, for Dick, the health problem of diabetes. Ruby turned to Charlotte (Mrs. Lyle) Stanford and Mrs. Mabel Coddington, two Caldwell neighbors, for help. The former was an experienced public school teacher with special training in reading and spelling; the latter was a professor of education at the local college.

It was no easy task to persuade Charlotte Stanford to take the job. Stanford family tradition tells of Ruby's offers of a good stipend and Lottie's demurral, saying it isn't the money; it's the time it takes. Now, the family story goes, if she could just get some help with her ironing, she might have time to help. Lottie's husband was a professor at the college, there were several youngsters in school, and the family ironing was altogether too demanding for Lottie to take on such a job as Ruby had in mind. Ruby, according to the story, solved that problem by doing the ironing herself.[3]

However, neither Lottie nor Mabel was able to help the boys, and private schools were sought as a final recourse.

Dick and Don were probably dyslexic. That condition has been so frequently studied and written about since the Simplot boys were small that pop psychology makes it easily overapplied. It is possible that the boys were like their father in this respect. That is, it may be that Jack's lifelong difficulities with spelling and his slow reading reveal dyslexia or a tendency toward it.[4]

The boys were sent to Ojai, California, and enrolled in private school there, Don entrusted with the formidable task of monitoring the diabetes restrictions laid upon his older brother. Private prep schools in the East were selected to finish the boys' pre-college education, Dick going to Oxford Academy in Atlantic City, New Jersey, Don enrolling at Warren School in Olney, Maryland.

Don Simplot remembers those days:

I was held back two years, so consequently I was quite a bit bigger and older than most . . . and bored to death. Dad was never around. I never saw him, and Mother wasn't much of a disciplinarian . . . so we just kind of grew up . . . helter-skelter. So Dad eventually shipped my brother and [me] off to the Ojai Prep School, in Ojai, California. . . . we got in trouble in Ojai, and Dad shipped us to private school back in Washington, D. C.

I went to Warren School in Olney, Maryland, and my brother went to Oxford Academy in Atlantic City, New Jersey. . . . He was a diabetic, of course, so I became his guardian. And I don't know if that was good or not, but I had to give a report if he had any sugar or ate any candy bars or anything like that. . . . So anyway, through the tutors and through everything else, I went to The College of Idaho for three years, and then I quit. I didn't graduate. . . . I was on the football team., earned a letter. . . . I played with R. C. Owens and Buzz Bonaminio and all those guys. . . . I was never very good, but we had a pretty good team." [5]

Dick fought diabetes most of his life, a battle whose outcome was complicated by alcholism,[6] and died June 24, 1993. Richard Rosevear Simplot was fifty-nine. Before joining the corporate headquarters in Boise in 1960, he worked at the Gay Mine near Pocatello, Simplot Soilbuilders at Twin Falls, and at the Cal-Ida Lumber in Auburn, California. In August 1970, Dick Simplot became a member of the board of directors and was a vice president and director until his death.[7]

At the time of the interview, Don and his fifth wife were awaiting the birth of twins. He said he has six children by previous marriages. The oldest is forty-three.

After resting for ten years, the Simplot stork returned to active duty February 1, 1945, with the birth of Gay Corrine. She attended Washington Elementary School, North Junior High School, and Boise High, graduating in 1963.

Gay said during her childhood she was taught the value of money:

> *Dad was not too much a part of that* [upbringing]. *He was so busy building his empire . . . that family was the responsibility of Mom and, I guess, our—Scott's and my—governess, Florence Galvin. . . .*
>
> *I did not have a checking account, not until after I went to college. I did earn money in the summertime—$5 a week at McCall. My duties were dusting, vacuuming, and the windows . .*

. and the dusting had to be done every day, windows once a week, and so on. And during the wintertime we did receive an allowance, but I can't remember how much or what we did . . . . Basically, [we] *were taught a respect for money. If* [we] *made a wager,* [we] *were taught to make good on* [it], *no matter how much it hurt. . . .*

Gay said the age gap between her and older brothers, Dick and Don, was significant:

. . . I don't know that I was very close to my oldest brother [Dick] *at all because he had different interests, but I am somewhat close to Don.* [He and my ex-husband] *were very good friends.*

Gay's first year of post-high school education was at Colorado Women's College, after which she studied at The College of Idaho. She said it took a while to get on track academically:

The first two years were very difficult for me. So the first two years, nah. But once I got into my major, I really, really loved it!

My major was biology. . . . I did take geology . . . It was wonderful. I never worked so hard for a 'C' in my life, but I loved it.[8]

Gay married C. L. "Butch" Otter in 1964. They later divorced. She has four children who range in age from thirty to twenty-three.

Scott Robert Simplot, the youngest of J. R. and Ruby's children, was born in 1946. He, too, attended Washington Elementary, North Junior High, and Boise High schools, graduating in 1964. It was taken for granted that he would go to college, and the school of his choice was the University of Idaho. Modest about his academic accomplishments, he nevertheless was admitted into the graduate program of one of the finest business schools in the nation, the University of Pennsylvania's Wharton School. Scott remembers:

> *I was thirteen when I got my first summer job. . . . It was one of those great things in life. I got to keep the money from that summer. I obviously had my needs taken care of well enough, even though there wasn't an allowance. But you know I put that money into Idaho Power. That was the first stock I bought,* [and] *once or twice a year* [Dad would ask], *"How ya doin', son?" He had an interest there, how I was doing with my stocks.*
>
> *He* [J. R.] *had a cattle ranch . . . in Nevada, so I went down there for . . . I bet it was maybe five or six weeks that first summer. . . . The next summer it was maybe two months on the ranch and one month in McCall, then ten weeks on the ranch and two weeks in McCall by the time I got to be in high school. .*
>
> *We had a war on at the time* [when Scott was in college] *. . . and they dropped graduate deferments. My Commander-in-Chief was Richard Milhous Nixon. I got drafted, . . . spent two years in the army . . . hooked up to*

another year at Wharton, went back and finished up, . . .earning an MBA in Management Information Systems, which is sort of a computer accounting.[9]

Scott married while still in college. He and his wife had two daughters before they divorced after fourteen years. In 1999 he remarried.

In 1960, after twenty-nine years of marriage, Ruby Simplot left Jack, seeking and obtaining a divorce so she could marry the husband of a friend, a man with whom she had fallen in love. Of the parting, Ruby said:

You know, I had an album of things when I left Jack, [but] *I didn't want that part of my history any more, I guess. But I don't know why, because I had nothing really against Jack. It was just that I thought really and truly that we had many things that we could talk about, differences; but it just came to the place that he was getting so involved and he loved the people that he would meet in New York or Chicago or whatever he was doing. It was great. And I wanted the sticks, you know. And so forth. Therefore I thought, "He wants to be up here, and I want to stay right down here." But then we had other differences, of course, too.*[10]

And those differences proved to be irreconcilable. Consequently, on July 1, 1960, and with apparently no hesitation Ruby left the Simplot McCall, Idaho home, went to Boise and from there to Nevada. It was left for Jack to inform the children, at least the fourteen- and fifteen-year-old Scott and Gay, of their mother's decision and to pick up the fragments of domestic life at 1500 Harrison Boulevard as best he could.

Jack described the settlement as follows:

> *I made her a deal that I'd put a half million dollars in a trust in Nevada, and I did, which worked out great . . . . And she stayed with him three-four years and divorced him, and I don't know what . . . happened. But she's still got the trust, and I put some good stocks there, and I . . . don't know . . . I think they've made her rich.*[11]

In *The Spirit of Enterprise*, George Gilder writes:

"A man of stern frontier morality, taught at his mother's knee, Simplot was no philanderer. But like many entrepreneurs with strong committments to family and society (major entrepreneurs are rarely bachelors), Simplot . . . performed an act of violation and adultery: he married his company and its problems. Left too frequently alone Rosie [Ruby] left Simplot, deepening his sense of guilt and his drive to prove himself in the face of a doubting father and a departing wife. A new crisis of breaking away unleashed in Simplot, as in so many other divorced entrepreneurs, a furious compulsion to rebuild his company and retrieve a family."[12]

It wasn't until January 22, 1972, that Jack's nearly ten-year bachelor existence ended when he married Esther Becker of Omro, Wisconsin. They had met in New York City, where Esther was a receptionist on the executive floor at the Henry Phipps Foundation, having worked in the City for almost ten years.

Esther described her first encounter with Jack:

> [Mr. Phipps] *had made his money in the steel business with Andrew Carnegie. This office handled the money for all the heirs of Henry Phipps, of which there were a considerable number. . . . The elevator opened one day, and this man with his volume on high stepped off the elevator. And I thought . . . everybody thought . . . "What is this?" But he had an appointment with Mr. Kingsley, our president, and Mr. Kingsley was late.*
>
> *So part of my job as receptionist was to chat with people if they didn't want to read, or if they wanted to converse. It was part of my job to be polite, and then he went in to talk to Mr. Kingsley. When he came out, he asked for the United Airlines number. He made me a little nervous, so I looked it up in the phone book, and I gave him the cargo number. And he knew all along what the number was because he said, "That's not right." So he just tried to challenge me a little bit, and I think make some conversation, but he laughed. And then later on he called me and invited me out to a show and supper. So I gambled. I'm not a gambler as a rule, but I thought, "Well, why not?". . .*

We went to a show, and he didn't like it, so we left in the middle of it and went out and had some supper . . . I think it was at the Waldorf Astoria. And then he took me home, and I didn't see him for another year.

And then he came in. . . blew in. . . and called me again. I said, "Well, another show, another dinner." I was working hard and studying and really poor so a show and dinner was a real treat. So we went to Hello, Dolly! *and he slept through the whole thing! At that point I said (to myself), "Maybe I'd better disassociate myself from this particular man."*

And it wasn't until later that I found out that he was betting on the potato futures and that he was trying to get hold of ninety-three cars of potatoes or something like that. And he'd been up for two or three days and was absolutely exhausted. But it was years later before I knew and understood what he was doing. I didn't know a potato future from a potato plow or anything else; so needless to say, I was not very impressed at that point.

. . . So it just continued. He'd come to town infrequently, and maybe we'd go to the movie or something. And then in about . . . I would say '68 he invited me to come to Idaho, and things became much more serious . . . . I finally moved to Denver because commuting from New York got to be a real chore.

I worked for a brokerage company in Denver; it was called Dominick and Dominick . . . .I was there about two years. I think I left New York in '68. . . . I stayed here for a while

> *and things didn't materialize, and I could understand that a man of his means. . .would naturally have to be very careful about remarrying. . . .So after a period of time I just decided that maybe I wasn't the right one, and I decided to go to Indiana University. And then he decided maybe I was the right one, so after that I came back for Christmas, and we were married in January . . . January 22, 1972, in McCall at his lodge.*[13]

In one of life's twists and turns, Jack Simplot had met a young—she was born in 1934—Wisconsin farm girl in New York City, and she has proved to be his steady companion for twenty-eight years. Like Jack, she attended a country school (one room), shocked grain, worked in the hay, hoed potatoes, and milked cows. Electricity reached the Becker home when she was eight years old. A bright youngster, she was valedictorian of her high school graduating class and active in nearly all aspects of school life, including musical and other extra-curricular activities. Remembering her elementary and high school teachers with much affection, Esther graduated *magna cum laude* from MacMurray College in Jacksonville, Illinois, with a major in voice and music education. She taught school in Lincolnwood, Illinois, for two years before going to New York for further study.

There is no question Esther filled a void in Jack's life. Twenty-eight years later, he called their marriage one of the best things he had ever done.[14]

Chapter Ten Notes

1. JRS, 11-18-98, tape 1, side B.

2. RRS, 7-29-99, tape 1, side A.

3. This version of Ruby, Lottie, and the ironing-for tutoring was collected from Janice (Mrs. John) Stanford Burch, Summer, 1999. When Ruby was asked whether she could verify the account, she replied that she could not remember ironing clothes for Lottie, although she would have been happy to do so if it would have helped the boys. (July 29, 1999) Jack says, "I don't know if it was the second or third grades [that] I could see they weren't getting anywhere, and I said, 'Well, hell, let's put 'em in private school,' and we did. They went to private school, both the older boys—California—and then I sent Dick to a school in the East somewhere—Pennsylvania, was it? Cost me ten or fifteen thousand dollars a year, a pretty nice school . . . . " 9-18-98, tape 2, side A.

4. Respecting the possibility that Jack may himself be dyslexic, perhaps an unrecognized and hence unspoken sympathy brought together Jack Simplot and Nelson Rockefeller, a well known sufferer from dyslexia. Jack said, "I'm still pretty good with figures. Spelling was my big downfall, and when I started running my own business I just ran into a wall in spelling . . . . I never could spell worth a damn." JRS interview, 9-24-98, tape 3, side B. Adelia Garro Simplot in an interview with the author on May 12, 2000, observed that Jack may well be dyslexic and speculates that this condition has had genetic consequences.

5. DJS, 1-26-2000, tape 1, side B. Don did not think that he was named after the hero Don John of Austria, celebrated in Chesterton's poem "Lepanto," who helped halt a Turkish sea invasion and saved European culture in the sixteenth century.

6. Serwer, "Wildest Billionaire," 8.

7. Simplot "Newsletter," Winter, 1993-94, 3.

8. GCS, 1-26-2000, tape 1, side A. Gay was formerly married to C. L. "Butch" Otter.

9. SRS, 1-26-2000, tape 1, side A.

10. RRS, 8-29-99, tape 1, side A. By the assertion "He wants to be up here, and I want to stay right down here," Ruby apparently refers to the position or place in society occupied by people of wealth who are concomitantly people of power and high visibility.

11. In two separate interviews (October 15 and November 18, 1998) Jack discussed the divorce, and it was clear that it was one of the profoundly painful experiences of his life. Yet he was unsure that he wanted its details to be a

part of his biography ("I don't know that I want it to be mentioned. Yes, something about it. What the hell . . . . ") He said, further, "I had no idea of that woman ever leaving me. We got along [well].; we never had a bit of trouble, and I never—hell—I . . . stepped out with nobody! Nobody!" The break came at a particularly bad time, just as he was about to close a fifteen million dollar loan with a Boston insurance company. Left with the care of two adolescent children, Jack was fortunate to have their nanny, Florence "Flory" Galvin, continue in his employ. Of the dissolution of the marriage, son Don Simplot says, "When they got divorced, that was a traumatic deal in Dad's life. . . . I'd travel with him a lot, and I knew a lot of his friends . . . but Dad was so involved in business he didn't have time [to philander]. I mean he was thinking about how he was going to get that next buck and how he was going to get that next ton of ore out of the ground or something like that . . . unbelievable. And so . . . when Mother finally ran off with this guy, Bob Jordan—fifteen years older than she was . . . that was a traumatic deal for Dad." DJS 1-26-2000, tape 1, side B.

12. 36.

13. EBS, 2-9-2000, tape 1, side A.

14. JRS, 2-14-2000, tape 1, side A.

Chapter Eleven

Passing the reins: Growth in the '70s and '80s

The decade of the 1970s saw a veritable welter of activities, changes, and growth, requiring nearly ten full pages of the *Chronology*. In the first year of the new decade, Simplot closed the Taber, Alberta, potato plant, and acquired nine new Soilbuilder units in Washington and Oregon, bringing to eighty the number of Simplot Soilbuilders units in farming country in twelve states between the Mississipi River and the Pacific Ocean. Personnel changes occurred this year as Simplot chose Jim Conrad to replace longtime Food Division president Leon Jones, who retired. John Dahl was chosen to serve as corporate executive vice president.

A major ($6.5 million) potato processing plant that had been projected for the San Luis Valley of Colorado was abandoned when a planning session in Caldwell concluded that future needs could be met by perfecting operations in Idaho.[1]

Simplot has observed that he situated his plants

beside streams so that he would have a handy place to dispose of his muck; while claiming that little damage was done to the environment, he nevertheless welcomed the regulations that made him clean up his operations, for he had no intention of polluting rivers.[2] He advocates the enforcement of environmental regulations as long as they are equally applied so that he can meet his competitors on equal terms. He had seen milky streams in foreign countries and has no desire to see America's watercourses similarly abused. Accordingly, the *Chronology* for 1971 includes the addition of three new cyclonic scrubbing systems to replace aging air pollution abatement facilities and the installation of an eliminator to eradicate emissions from the granulation plant at Pocatello. Further improvements included the installation of a spill control system, a tailgas cleaning system, a de-mister, and a 200-foot stack. More than that, the company completed a $2 million water treatment installation at the Burley-Heyburn plant.[3]

Nineteen seventy-two was thus a good year for Simplot, and 1973 held considerable promise as well, for it was this year that Jack passed the presidential reins of the company over to his hand-picked successor, John Dahl, whose contributions to the company had been of the first magnitude. Simplot described the changes for the Company History Project:

> *Well, he* [John Dahl] *knew more about my books than anybody else, and he'd earned his way with me . . . . John did us a good job, no question about it. Of course I still ran the com-*

pany practically, but I made them CEOs because I wanted to be Chairman of the Board, and I wanted them to take the responsibility . . . .

Simplot also picked Dale Dunn and Gordon Smith, the presidents who followed Dahl. Steve Beebe was selected by the new co-chairmen after Jack had vacated the chairmanship.

Oh, sure. Why naturally, I knew 'em, and I ran the company . . . up until I quit [as] *Chairman of the Board here in this last year* [1994] . . . .

All Simplot presidents have come from within the Simplot organization. Has Simplot ever considered bringing in a president from outside the company?

No, I haven't. Hell no. I want sombody that knows something about it. No, I haven't needed to bring anybody in, and I'm not going to as long as I'm around because I know these men. They've been with me all their lives, you know, and I know 'em. I know their abilities, and I know they're honest. [4]

In 1975 Jack made a major investment in a gold mine in the Dominican Republic. The *Chronology* describes it this way:

"Following an investment of $45 million, partnership of Simplot Industries/Rosario Resources/Central

Bank began extracting ore from the Dominican Republic gold and silver mine and began operating an 8,000 ton/day mill at Pueblo Viejo in Sanchez Ramirez Province; the first bars of "Dore" bullion were poured and shipped to Switzerland for refining and marketing."[5]

So the first half of the decade augured a future bright with promise: improvements and refinements in production with an eye to environmental accountability, the first of a succession of capable executives into whose hands new or added responsibliites were placed, a host of company activities, a bright marriage. But the second half of the 1970s had its downside.

Jack Simplot was charged in 1976 with manipulating the futures market in potatoes. Writer George Gilder describes it thus:

"He [Simplot] guessed a major move in the potato price and went short 1,400 futures contracts on the Commodities Exchange. As the closing day approached and the price dropped from $17 to $8, hundreds of traders faced ruin. In desperation, some apparently stirred up snarl and panic on Maine's potato markets and train lines to prevent delivery of potatoes that Simplot had contracted to provide. Fifty-five of the losers sued Simplot as the most prosperous available target."[5]

Gilder finds no merit in the charges that Simplot had manipulated the market:

"As the market . . . sustained Simplot's position, any theoretical manipulation must have occurred on the other side, among desperate holders of contracts to buy $8 potatoes for $17. But he had *failed* [italics in original] to make a portion of his contracted deliveries, and in the end, to avoid endless fighting in court 'against city hall,' [quotation marks in original] he had to settle a civil action before the Commodity Futures Trading Commission by agreeing to suspend trading for five years."[6]

In the second instance, J. R. Simplot and his company were charged with violating income tax laws. Specifically, according to the *Idaho State Journal* of Wednesday, May 4, 1977, Simplot was charged with a count of filing a false tax return for 1970; three counts of assisting in the filing of false corporate returns for the J. R. Simplot Company for 1970, 1971, and 1972; the company and Simplot Industries, four counts of filing false corporate returns for those three years. All were felonies, to which Simplot entered a plea of no contest.

For his offenses, Simplot paid a fine of $40,000 and, according to a video tape prepared by the Special Affairs Department of Boise's KTVB News, lost his right to vote in presidential elections. He is recorded on the tape saying, "I had lots of pockets, and I paid out of the wrong pockets, but they were all my pockets."[7]

These setbacks prompt a couple of observations about his character. In a conversation about politics, Jack said:

> *I stayed away from politics. I didn't get involved. I decided a long time ago, "Why choose up sides? You're gonna have to get along with whoever's in there." So that's been my policy . . . . Nobody knew whether I was a Republican or a Democrat, and I never went one time over there* [to the seat of government] *and asked anybody for anything. I say you put 'em in there to run it; let 'em run it. I've got my hands full where I'm at . . . . I guess I've always been a Republican, but I never admitted it, and I helped the Democrats. I helped the good people that I thought were gonna help Idaho.*[8]

It would be difficult to find a more pragmatic view of politics, and it is Jack Simplot to the core.

The second observation brings to mind a story by Edward Everett Hale, once popular in the public school curriculum of America. The account of the fictional Lt. Philip Nolan of "The Man Without a Country" contrasts remarkably with the disposition of the real Jack Simplot, who never once faltered in his love affair with America.

One might suppose that Simplot, on the losing side in two tussles with Uncle Sam, might look with rancor and cynicism at the interference of government in his affairs (one can almost hear the cracker barrel philosophers vituperate about "the dadblamed guvment" while they spit tobacco juice into the heating stove at the country store), but there was none of that. Whereas Philip Nolan cried, "Damn the United States! I wish I may never hear of the United States again!" and lived out his sentence on warships, never hearing of or seeing his country again, Jack Simplot bought an American flag thirty feet by fifty feet and attached it to his flagpole at his hilltop home overlooking Boise, where it announces that here dwells a patriot.[9]

Gamblers are realists who know that there are times when bad hands will be dealt, and Jack is nothing if not a gambler. Losses will occur, in the nature of things. If you can't take them, don't gamble. Some of this attitude may have helped forestall the development of cynicism, a characteristic totally foreign to his make up.

In his facing up to the charges in both instances, Simplot contrasts sharply with the grandfather of his friend Nelson Rockefeller, for John D., Senior, in 1879, launched a thirty-year period as a fugitive from justice, cleverly avoiding indictments which would have brought the miscreant monopolist to trial.[10]

In July 1978, John Dahl retired as company president and was succeeded in that position by A. Dale Dunn, whose place as president of the Minerals and Chemical Division was assumed by Ben McCollum. Simplot's judgment in both instances was vindicated. The next year, 1979, saw a busy Simplot and Company forming Simplot International, a wholly owned subsidiary, whose mission was to provide help and capital in Argentina and parts of Europe where potatoes were grown. Jack's international activities were disrupted when the Dominican Republic nationalized the gold mine in which he had invested, a sharp downturn for the industrialist, for the mine was grossing an estimated $1 million per day. The Dominican Republic Central Bank bought the interests of Simplot and Rosario—twenty-seven percent each—in the mine.[11] Taped conversations capture Simplot's reflections about this mine:

> *Yeah, and it* [the gold mine] *was a dandy. . . . Put $80 million down there, and we got it all back the first year . . . in one mine. Of course, gold went to $800 an ounce, and I think we ran it three years and the third year they just came and said . . . . they'd had the hurricane, and the government was broke, and the president called us in and said, "Fellas, that's the only cash cow we've got, and we've got to have it. So I'll tell you what we'll do. We'll give you seventy-five million dollars cash and that's it." So we took the $75 million.*[12]

Besides the coconut plantation mentioned earlier, Simplot also had three plywood lathes and eleven sawmills in operation on the coast of Columbia, all of which he ultimately abandoned with a loss of $30 million because he was unwilling to put up with kidnapping, extortion, and bribery. His experience with a nickel mine in this country is illustrative:

> *I found a big nickel mine down there . . . best nickel mine in the world. And I took it* [the title claims] *to the Supreme Court, and I won it in the Supreme Court in Columbia, and I couldn't get it.* [The case] *went through three presi-*

dents, and they wouldn't give me that nickel mine without $700,000 or a million dollars under the table. And I decided I wouldn't pay it, and I didn't. The last president—now these were [four or six year terms]—*gave it back to the people we beat, and it was Standard Oil Company. They bribed their way in there and took that . . . nickel mine away from me after I won it in the Supreme Court! Shows you how tough it is down there.*[13]

A bright spot in 1979 was the launching of what would become the annual sponsorship of the Simplot Games, a track and field meet for high school athletes at Pocatello, Idaho. Many observers have commented on Simplot's athletic appearance and his durable physique, and it is true that his interest in athletics has been lifelong. He also sponsored a successful AAU basketball team, and radio commentator Lowell Thomas in a 1957 broadcast from Sun Valley described him as "built like a Notre Dame fullback" and "a good-natured giant."[14] The sponsor's athleticism combined with his philanthropic nature in the creation of the Simplot Games made the event one of the premiere spring meets in the nation.

Although the decade of the 1970s was a mixture of dark and light, success and failure, Simplot still made money and never for a second thought of giving up in despair. He had survived two major shocks. He had had opportunities to sell everything, to close out his operations to well known and respected firms. But as he often says, if his outfit—or his rig—was worth that much to somebody else, it was worth more to him. So he hung on through the 1970s and continued to make money. And his judgment was as sound as ever as shown in the selection of the new presidents.

Of the eleven activities that launched the new decade, one stands out: the expansion of the mining capabilities at the Conda Mine to the tune of $3 million, including the acquisition of a $1.6 million 17-cubic yard shovel, a $600,000 road grader, and a $950,000 Blast Hole Drill.[15] But the next year was even busier with nineteen discrete activities, accomplishments, ventures. It would appear that Jack was finding the capital to bring to life earth's concealed or overlooked resources.

A random selection from the activities for 1981 reveals the company acquired a potato processing plant at Grand Forks, North Dakota; a subsidiary of Simplot International bought a fifty percent interest in a Dutch corporation whose potato processing plant was located at Bergen op Zoom; the Pocatello fertilizer plant was awarded the top industrial award for 1981 for the entire state of Idaho by the Pacific Northwest Pollution Control Association for the plant's wastewater land project; and a $1.7 million wastewater processing and land treatment plant at Hermiston, Oregon was completed. Near the right hand margin of this page of the *Chronology* under the heading of Misc. Notes/Comments is an eight word sentence that is so modest it could easily be overlooked: "First computer chips are produced by Micron Technology."[16]

If it is accurate to say that with the production of dried potatoes and onions during World War II Simplot became a millionaire and that when his fertilizer operations and the McDonald's connection took off he reached multi-millionaire status, then his success with Micron made him a billionaire.

It was Simplot's youngest son, Scott, who got his father interested in the company being formed by brothers Joe and Ward Parkinson. Scott described how he persuaded Jack, who had built an empire on pigs and potatoes, to enter the highly speculative work of making computer chips:

> *Ron Yanke, Tom Nicholson, and Allen Noble* [local farmers and businessmen] *came in here and sat down and talked to me for twenty minutes and said, "Gee, you want to talk to Ward Parkinson." I agreed. . . and Ward pitched the notion that "Look, I can do the design on a DRAM memory chip. Oh, by the way, I have a guy who's very skillful in laying this out, and his name is Doug Pitman. And by the way I have another engineer who's named Dennis Wilson, who can do the simulation. And you know, the three of us are very capable of coming up with a viable design for making a 64 chip." And that seemed to ring true to me. It was like, "Well of course these guys can . . . they're doing it. They've done it once . . . .They're really capable of doing it again." So that might be step one.*
>
> *Step two was a general sense that this was*

important; that this was a great, bright future for personal computers, computers in general. That [insight] *is just a product of my [educational] background. Yes, the beacon was on . . . . At this point I got excited, and I went to my father and said, "We've got to do this." And I don't know . . . I can't say I had a hard sell. The first time he heard it he wasn't too interested, but I don't think it was twenty-four hours later that . . . you know . . . something triggered in him so he was willing to sit down and listen . . . and he jumped on it.*[17]

Indeed he did. With both feet. For forty percent of what blossomed into Micron Technology, Jack Simplot gave the Parkinson brothers $1 million, and when the fledgling chip maker required more, he invested another $20 million.

A story in the *Idaho Statesman* puts it this way:

"Simplot, who doesn't type or use a computer, pumped in $20 million more to help Micron build its first fabrication plant and to stay afloat."[18]

In those early days of its life, Simplot owned or controlled the largest single block of Micron stock, but he has gradually reduced his holdings until he now—as of April 30, 1999—owns about eight million shares while J. R. Simplot Company owns about thirteen million shares.[19] Because of the wide and sometimes wild divagations of the stock market, it is very difficult (some would say impossible) to specify precisely a

An obviously proud Jack Simplot poses with his first-born child, Dick.

Simplot family album

J. R. Simplot Co. archives

J. R. Simplot Co. archives

John Sokol, president of Sokol & Company, met Jack Simplot by accident in Burbank, California, in 1941 and became Simplot's first processed-food client.

J. R. Simplot Co. Archives

Workers pose around Simplot's first electric potato sorter. Jack's brother Bob is at far right.

J. R. Simplot Co. Archives

Simplot's first onion dryer began operation in the new Caldwell, Idaho plant in October 1941. Below, John Bowers, Jr. moves a tray of onions to the drying line.

J. R. Simplot Co. archives

During the war years, Simplot's Caldwell, Idaho, plant operated around the clock. The workforce grew from 100 to 1,200. Simplot had to start his own box factory (below) to ship the containers of dehydrated onions and potatoes.

J. R. Simplot Co. archives

Leon Jones joined Simplot in 1942 to oversee government contracts. He became the driving force behind the growth of the food division.

J. R. Simplot Co. archives

R. Starr Farish was Simplot's first professional sales manager. After the war he organized the expansion into frozen french fry market.

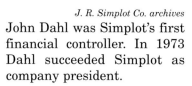

J. R. Simplot Co. archives

John Dahl was Simplot's first financial controller. In 1973 Dahl succeeded Simplot as company president.

J. R. Simplot Co. archives

Jack Simplot speaks during ceremonies at the Caldwell, Idaho, plant on January 8, 1944. The company received the War Department's E-award for excellence in wartime production.

Simplot family album

A Simplot family Christmas card, circa 1950, obviously staged by the photographer. Jack, left, watches as Ruby reads a Christmas story to Gay and Scott. Sons Don and Dick appear engrossed in a game of checkers.

J. R. Simplot Co. archives

By the end of the war, Idaho had a national reputation for its potatoes, largely due to products produced by Jack Simplot's company.

Simplot family album

Jack, Ruby and daughter Gay in 1958, on Gay's thirteenth birthday.

Photo courtesy Micron Technology

Simplot was instrumental in the founding of Micron Technology, one of the nation's largest manufacturers of computer memory. Micron is one of the area's largest employers. Micron's success pushed Simplot from multi-millionaire to billionaire.

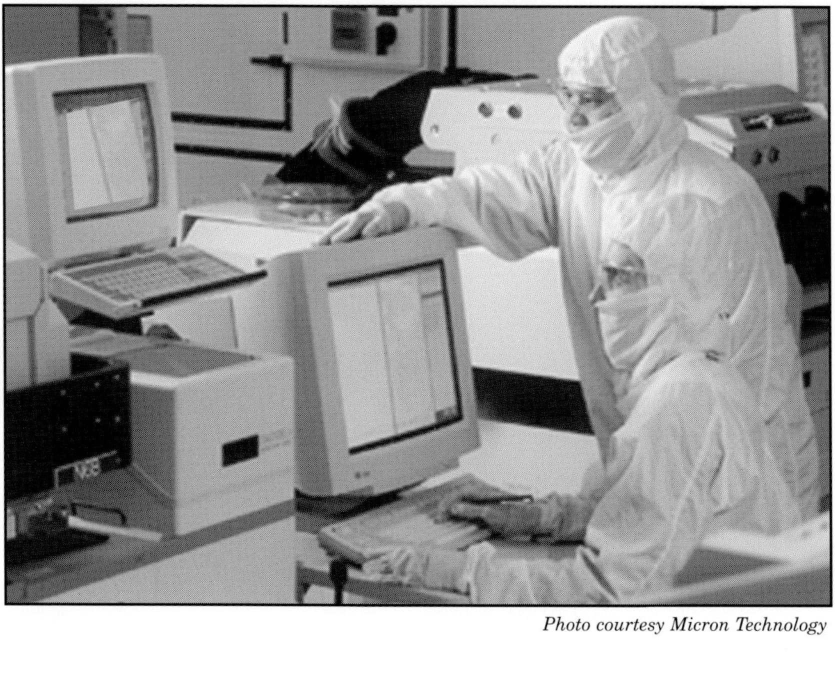

Photo courtesy Micron Technology

Wayne Cornell

Still going strong in his nineties, Simplot talks excitedly about a new project during an aerial tour of his plants, while Esther Simplot (background) reads a newspaper.

Wayne Cornell

Simplot discusses cattle prices with Tom Basabe, manager of the Grand View, Idaho, livestock operation. Tom's father, John, played a key role in starting the feedlot. Below, J. R. interupts his tour to say hello to Basabe's daughter, Mila, left, and her friend, Shenna Draper, who were painting fence.

Wayne Cornell

The Simplot phosphate refining plant at Rock Springs, Wyoming.

Wayne Cornell

Phosphate from the Smoky Canyon Mine on the Idaho-Wyoming border is turned into a slurry and pumped through a pipeline to a refining plant eighty-seven miles away in Pocatello, Idaho.

Wayne Cornell

"Hi. I'm Old Man Simplot!" Jack greets an employee during a tour of the Smoky Canyon Mine. Below, he stands in the room in the Caldwell, Idaho, plant where the first onion dehydrator went into operation in October 1941. He helped install the equipment.

Wayne Cornell

It takes five people to maintain the "lawn" around the Simplot home in the foothills above Boise, Idaho. Some of his neighbors complained that when his thirty- by fifty-foot American Flag snapped in the wind, it sounded like gunshots.

Wayne Cornell

The Simplot company logo includes a sombrero—the type of hat worn by the founder in his youth.

Wayne Cornell

Jack and Esther Simplot

person's wealth or financial ranking at any given moment. That doesn't stop *Forbes* magazine, however, for that journal didn't hesitate to estimate Simplot's wealth at $2.5 billion, tieing him for the distinction of being the 130th wealthiest person in the United States, with the J. R. Simplot Company listed as 42nd among the 500 largest private companies.[20] Bob Eure writing in the Sunday *Oregonian* said, "*Fortune* magazine last year (1995) ranked him as the thirty-seventh wealthiest American, his wealth pegged at $2.2 billion."[21]

But that's getting ahead of the story.

Activities of Simplot and his firm for the years 1980-89 require fifteen pages in the *Chronology*. The history of the company, its subsidiaries, and its joint ventures is also the story of Jack Simplot. It was his energy, his drive, his judgment, and his optimistic view of the world of possibilities that had created the firm. The firm is the objective correlative of the man, and it is difficult if not downright unrealistic to try to separate the creator from his creature.

In 1982, the company began operation of a $1.3 million garbage-fueled steam plant at the Heyburn potato processing plant, "meeting about ten percent of the overall steam requirements and used primarily in peeling and blanching operations."[22] Other developments were even more impressive, the completion of a $45 million expansion of the Brandon fertilizer plant, for instance, nearly doubling its capacity, and nearly tripling the capacity of the Overton, Nevada, silica complex through a $5 million expansion and updating.

Particularly exciting was launching the construction preliminary to opening the Smoky Canyon Mine near Afton, Wyoming, which would be called into service when the phosphate deposits at Conda were exhausted.[23] It began operations in 1984, the same year the company became the majority partner of the Cargill-Dufrit potato processing plant in Germany, renaming it Simplot Europe, while at the same time Simplot International became co-owner of a potato processing plant in Izmir, Turkey.

A major investment in the Pocatello fertilizer plant—$50 million—modernized and expanded that facility, assuring a thirty-five percent increase in phosophoric acid capacity and a new plant for producing sulfuric acid. Always alert to the economies of production as has been said, Simplot started a ninety-four-megawatt co-generation unit at the Helm, California, fertilizer plant by which $1.4 million for natural gas expenses and an additional $1 million for electricity would be saved annually. It was this year that the Smoky Canyon phosphate mine complex began operation, a project which, by 1991, would convey phosphate slurry through a remarkable underground pipeline system some eighty-seven miles from Smoky Canyon and the Conda Mine to Pocatello for processing.[24]

In 1987 the firm built a wastewater treatment plant for its operation at Hermiston, Oregon, for $2.5 million, and commenced a similar project for the Heyburn, Idaho, complex. Further reduction of environmental problems occurred that year when the plant at Lathrop, California, installed a gas-to-gas heat exchanger and added a second emissions absorption tower. President A. Dale Dunn meant what he said: "We must constantly and forever improve our approach to production and service, seek(ing) to do better what we already do quite well."[25]

Obviously one of the most important elements in this large matter of production about which President Dunn was speaking is the producers. The labor force, not just such matters as the technologies of production and the access to raw materials, must be improved. Jack Simplot saw this clearly many years ago when he sponsored an anti-smoking campaign by sending a speaker to schools. Equipped with photographs of damaged lungs, slides, microscopes, lung tissue samples, and other persuasive evidence of the violence smoking does to the lungs, Simplot's speaker tried to counter the human damage created by what he viewed as a deplorable habit.

Simplot's concerns about smoking did not diminish over the years. Accordingly, in 1988 a no-smoking policy in all company indoor facilities was implemented. Simplot is quoted as saying: "That's our policy. That's just it. And if they want to fight me on it, let 'em come."[26] As he says in the videotape of the 1982 television production *King of the Hill*, over the years he had witnessed too many of his friends let this addiction and whiskey destroy their lives.

Because of Simplot's well known abstemiousness, he is often thought to be a Mormon, the Latter-Day Saints having pre-empted the niche once occupied by the Methodist Church in respect to the use of alcohol. He is not a Mormon, however. In this connection, his now deceased friend and fellow billionaire Joe Albertson was often assumed to be a Mormon, perhaps because he was thought to have originated in Idaho. He was not.

Not all Simplot ventures are successful. In 1988 Simplot built an aquaculture facility at Caldwell for the raising of tilapia, a tropical fish that showed promise of providing a wholesome source of protein. Tilapia appeared to fit in with the economies-of-production orientation of the company, feeding, it was hoped, on some of the by-products of french fry production and converting that kind of waste into delectable fillets.

Try as they might, the staff could not make the fish experiment work and the project was later abandoned. However, good news countered the difficulties with tilapia culture when awards were forthcoming for work done to control water pollution. Both the Pacific Northwest Pollution Control Association and the Environmental Protection Agency recognized the company for making the most significant contribution to controlling water pollution in Idaho and the Northwest for 1988. This was also the year that the company motto with its implied mission statement was promulgated: "Bringing Earth's Resources To Life."

In December 1998, company president A. Dale Dunn retired and was replaced by Gordon Smith, and in the Land and Livestock Division John Basabe retired, replaced by his son Tom Basabe, who was named vice president and general manager of the Agriculture Group.[27]

A final item for this decade notes that savings of $500,000 per year were realized at Hermiston, Oregon, and Heyburn, Idaho by incinerating a by-product of wastewater treatment and using the energy for the task of processing.[28]

And these are only a few of the many and varied activities and developments of the company for this ten-year period. Major changes were in the wind for the next decade.

Chapter Eleven Notes

1. Simkins, 28.

2. "Jack Simplot: King of the Hill," KTVB News video tape, May 10,1982.

3. Simkins, 29.

4. Dec. 13, 1995.

5. Simkins, 33.

6. *The Spirit of Enterprise*, 39-40. In the *Fortune* cover story "Wildest Billionaire in the West," (Nov. 27, 1995) Andrew E. Serwer says that Simplot was barred from trading for six years, paid a fine of $50,000, and settled a civil suit for $1.4 million. (7)

7. *King of the Hill.* If invoked, this denial of the privilege of voting expires after five years, according to some authorities.

8. JRS 9-24-98, tape 4, side A.

9. If there is disagreement on the dimensions of the flag, one wonders how there can ever be agreement on profound and complicated matters, like the structure and function of a quark, for example. J. R. says the flag is 65'x30' (10-20-98, tape 1, side B); Steve Jenning says it is 50x30 (*Northwest Magazine, Oregonian*, Oct. 20, 1985); Kristen Moulton says it is 60x30 (*Idaho Statesman,* 11 April 1999). The thirty-foot dimension is constant; the average of the other three is 58.333.

10. Chernow, *Titan*, 212.

11. Simkins, *Chronology*, 36-37.

12. 9-24-98, tape 4, side A.

13. ibid.

14. Broadcasting from the Harriman residence in Sun Valley on March 8, 1957, Lowell Thomas dealt with the news of the day, and then in a portion of the broadcast near the end titled Yellowstone Lake he celebrated his most recent discovery in language somewhat intemperate as far as Jack's physical attributes are concerned: "Here at Sun Valley, on famous Mount Baldy I've been trying in vain to keep up with a rugged citizen of Idaho. I'd like to tell you a little about him. It seems to me he could be built up into quite an inspiration for the youth of America. His name is Jack Simplot, from Boise! Built like a Notre Dame fullback, he is one of the outstanding personalities of the West, head of an empire that includes tens of thousands of acres of sheep country, more tens of thousands of acres over which he and his associates run cattle. He owns gold mines, uranium mines and other mines where they get those new rare metals that are so valuable in this jet—atom-

ic age. He has deposits of iron, sulphur, manganese, and almost everything you can imagine.

"You would think it would be difficult to build up such a diversified empire. But not for a good-natured giant like Jack Simplot, who obviously knows how to pick people, and then let them take over."

He has a paragraph on Jack and potatoes, followed by a brief paragraph on his education, his knowledge, and his judgment, followed by, "As he goes banging down these Saw Tooth [sic] mountains on skis, you can hear him singing and laughing, half a mile away." Although the next three paragraphs merit citation because they deal with a subject vital to Simplot industries, the American West, and indeed the entire planet—water—only one will be offered here:

"Jack Simplot thinks big. As you know, one of the great problems in much of the West is the problem of water. His latest suggestion is that a way be found to raise the water level of Yellowstone Lake. He says this would be fairly easy. Then, all that surplus water, in the spring, to be piped East, down through Wyoming into my old state of Colorado, to a part of Colorado that has had at least two grim dust bowl experiences."

This portion of the broadcast ends with "You meet people like that out here at Sun Valley."

The broadcast was transcribed, yielding a slightly different text, and is filed in the corporation headquarters in Boise.

15. Chronology, 38. Of his pride in ownership and reluctance to sell, journalist Bob Eure writing in "Ridin' High with J. R. Simplot," the *Sunday Oregonian*, quotes Simplot: "I love my damn business. It's mine. It's real. And nobody ever put a dollar into it but me. I'll never sell it." (June 30, 1996)

16. 39.

17. SRS 1-26-2000, Side A.

18. April 11, 1990.

19. *Idaho Statesman*, April 30, 1999.

20. *Idaho Statesman*, April 4, 1999.

21. "Ridin' High with J. R. Simplot," June 30, 1996.

22. *Chronology*, 41.

23. ibid.

24. *Chronology*, 44, 56. As indicated in the introductory remarks, a visit to the Smoky Canyon Mine convinces the skeptic that both the industrialist and his enterprise are first magnitude. The earth-moving equipment is huge with shovels into which a house would fit dumping hundreds of tons of phosphate-bearing earth into trucks whose size intimidates the imagination. The

slurry pipeline carrying a mixture of water—40 percent—and phosphate with an internal pressure varying from 100 to 3200 psi, depending on the elevation, reduces transportation costs and the associated environmental distress while increasing production by 20 percent. At the end of the process, the water is recycled and the overburden replaced when the deposit has been mined. Herds of elk graze on the reclaimed land.

25. *Chronology*, 46-47.

26. In Bunderson, *Idaho Entrepreneurs*, 31.

27. *Chronology*, 50-52.

28. *Chronology*, 52

Chapter Twelve

From the heights

There is a hat incorporated in the Simplot Company logo. It is not just a hat; it is a Western sombrero, the kind of hat young Jack Simplot wore when he was working cattle, the kind worn by movie stars in the days of silent films and early talkies, stars like Tom Mix, George O'Brien (whom Jack resembled), Buck Jones, and Ken Maynard. The world had changed dramatically since those days, but the hat was a symbol that the company and its founder hadn't forgotten their roots.

The decade of the 1990s was just as full, just as challenging, just as ripe with promise as all the other decades of life of the J. R. Simplot Company. And that life, we should remember, goes back to the days when a youthful Jack Simplot was growing and shipping potatoes in the 1930s. Now in his eighties, Jack thought seriously about how he wanted to pass his outfit—his "rig"—on to another generation.

By 1996 Simplot's rig had assumed the following

shape. It was in three parts—the J. R. Simplot Company, the Simplot Family Trust, and Micron Technology.

The first of these parts, the Company, was organized into five groups:

- the Corporate Group: cheese factories in Idaho, Wisconsin, and Washington; vegetable greenhouses in Idaho and Nevada; meat processing plants in Idaho and Alabama (largest supplier of patties to Burger King).

- the Food Group: two billion pounds of frozen french fries supplying more than half of McDonald's needs from six U. S. plants, one in Canada, one in Beijing; guacamole from Mexico, frozen fruits and vegetables from the U. S. and Mexico.

- the Agriculture Group: one of ten top suppliers of cattle and beef in U. S. with feedlots in Oregon, Washington, and Idaho; several ranches including the ZX in Oregon at 1.3 million acres, the nation's largest.

- the Minerals and Chemical Group: phosphate and agricultural fertilizer outlets in sixteen states and Canada; phosphate mines in Utah and Idaho; a sand silica mine in Nevada; natural gas reserves in Alberta, Canada; Best Brand fertilizer sold wholesale and, through 100 Simplot Soilbuilders outlets, retail in the American West, Canada, and Mexico.

- the Diversified Group: the company's transportation arm in excess of 150 trucks and 600 railroad cars, and Western Stockman, a supplier of animal feed and nutritional supplements, including a sales component marketing dried beans, seeds, and pet foods.

The second part of his outfit was the Simplot Family Trust, which, in 1996, held ownership of real estate in Boise, including shopping centers, several blocks of the downtown area, and a subdivision. The trust also owned ten percent of Boise Cascade and Magma Copper Company.

The third part of his outfit was twenty-two percent of the stock of Micron Technology, one of the ten top producers of Dynamic Random Access memory chips for computers.[1]

All things considered it was quite a rig, created and sustained by the holder of an eighth grade diploma, a boy who had seen Buffalo Bill in the flesh, who had inadvertently hunted elk in Yellowstone Park (with legal consequences), who loved the outdoors and fishing and hunting and athletics, and who characterized himself in the TV documentary *King of the Hill* as a happy guy . . . never sick a day in his life . . . but no Houdini.

It was in the '90s that Joe Parkinson left Micron, the company he and his identical twin, Ward, had created. Writer Andrew Serwer explains the rift between J. R. and Joe in the following analysis for *Fortune* magazine.

According to Serwer, the high level of oversight maintained by the Micron board of directors was stifling to Joe, who was disinclined to accept micromanagement.

In the second place, Jack and Joe represented two personality extremes, Parkinson always preparing for the worst and Simplot always optimistic and expecting the best. Simplot therefore thought that Parkinson's communications to stockholders—Micron went public in 1984—were unduly pessimistic and faulted Joe for selling instead of hanging onto his stock.

Simplot and Parkinson also differed on whether and how to expand; hoarding profits and paying for expansion by stock issues as Joe wished would have diluted the stock, and Simplot did not approve.

The claim is also advanced that Parkinson feared that Simplot talked too much and revealed insider information "to his buddies down at the Arid Club and perhaps to Wall Street"; Parkinson therefore had Simplot sign an indemnification document pledging not to reveal inside information and to "'defend, hold harmless, and indemnify Micron' should he break the agreement."[2] This didn't sit well with Simplot, and Steve Appleton was chosen to replace Joe Parkinson when the rift became irreparable.

As is always the case when something dramatic like this occurs in a small community like Boise, the rupture was analyzed, suppled and driddled, talked over and written about extensively with an infinite variety of speculation. Serwer's analysis is as cogent as one is likely to find, as is his treatment of the Micron-

Simplot strategy for obtaining an engineering school for Boise State University.

As to how Simplot and Micron fit into this strategy, Serwer asserts that they—Simplot and Micron—leveraged an engineering school at Boise State University from the state government. Even after Simplot requested and got a joint meeting of the two houses of the state legislature and lectured them on the need for a local engineering school, there was still some resistance. Idaho is a thinly populated state and the University of Idaho, located in Moscow, already had an engineering school.

Micron on July 1, 1996, began to break ground near Lehi, Utah, with the implied threat of moving the Boise plant to a location near two schools of engineering which could presumably supply a ready cadre of engineers from universities—Utah and Brigham Young University—whose programs were accredited.[3] Resistance melted and Boise State got its engineering program.

The setting up of the family trust through which the Simplot empire will pass to his heirs occupied no insignificant portion of Jack's energy and attention, although, of course, its details and its language were the work of attorneys. The three surviving Simplot children, Don, Gay, and Scott comprise the living first generation of direct descendants whose children will ultimately benefit from the family trust, followed by the Simplot grandchildren, who are referred to as the "S-16."

Now a trust is an awesome thing. *Webster's Encyclopedic Unabridged Dictionary of the English*

Language (1989 edition) devotes an entire column—three columns to a page of characteristicaly small dictionary type—to a series of words and definitions all circling about the concept of trust, integrity, preservation, and responsibility. Reading all these, one is convinced that the concept of trust is one of the eternal verities right alongside truth, goodness, justice, and beauty. Jack Simplot explains the trust this way:

> *I've worked all my life for my family, you might say . . . , and I got an irrevocable trust started before they* [the lawmakers] *canceled* [the option]. *And . . . all of my stock's in it, and all of my former wife's stock's in it. And the only stock that's not in the trust is my kids' stock . . . and that's 65 . . .70 . . . 80 percent of the company is in this trust. And this trust won't trigger, maybe, for another fifty years, and when it triggers . . . my posterity own the company. They can do any damn thing they want, my posterity. And today, without it, you can't leave them anything, y'know, practically nothing: one of the third generation, 75* [percent]; *second generation, 55* [percent]. *You don't have a hell of a lot left. So . . . this big trust I got going is unique, real. All my grandkids have to do is keep it going, and they can build the thing as high as they want to build it. And when they get through, they have no taxes to pay or anything. The kids already own it. And it's something that I put together before they changed the laws; you can't have them any more.*[4]

One can imagine the baroque complexity of the legal language in which this trust arrangement is cast. But through its dark glass, Simplot's intention shines clear: he wants the integrity of the company preserved, he wants the ownership of the company clearly established, and he wants the transfer of ownership accomplished without tax penalty.

Richard Simplot's death in 1993 caused a tax dispute with the government, an argument that opened a window into the ownership of the company, the classes of stock by which that ownership was determined, and the value of the kinds of stock involved. A careful analysis of the matter by William M. Ringle, Gannett News Service, appeared in the *Idaho Statesman*, and we turn to it to broaden our understanding of the financial underpinnings of this powerful company.

The difficulty that faced both the company and the Internal Revenue Service was that of placing a dollar value on both the voting (class A) and the non-voting (class B) shares of stock, ownership shares that had never been sold and were not for sale. Ringle describes the company as "the closely-held J. R. Simplot Co., the agribusiness giant, which ranks 42nd on *Forbes* magazine's list of 500 private companies." Dick's estate set the value of the stock at $3,025 per share; the IRS set the value 265 times higher—$801,994 per share. U.S. Tax Court Judge Julian I. Jacobs faced two tasks: that of eliminating, or at least narrowing, the considerable gap; and that of deciding whether a voting share was worth more or the same as a non-voting share. The company said "worth the same," but the IRS said "worth more," and while both classes would pay the same dividend, the company had never (as of 1993) declared one.

Ringle takes this opportunity to offer a summary of Jack Simplot's wealth and accomplishments—produces two billion pounds of potatoes worth billions of dollars annually; makes billions more from interests in ranching, feedlots, chemicals, minerals, frozen fruits and vegetables, and computer chips (Micron): "Through affiliates, the corporation operates worldwide and employs about 12,000 persons. Revenues last year (1998) totaled about $2.8 billion."

In Dick's estate were eighteen shares of class A voting common stock in the family owned (private) corporation, constituting nearly a fourth (23.35 percent) of the outstanding voting stock. Also in the estate were 3,942 shares of non-voting class B stock, about 2.79 percent of the outstanding class B stock. The Gannett article states, "The remaining outstanding shares of class A voting stock were owned by Richard's sister, Gay C. Simplot, C. L. "Butch" Otter (then Gay's husband) and his brothers, Don J. and Scott R. Simplot. Virtually all of the class B non-voting shares were owned, directly or indirectly, by J. R. Simplot's descendants and by an employee stock ownership plan, ESOP, established in 1978)."

Both the estate and the IRS had outside experts supporting their positions. Judge Jacobs agreed with the IRS contention that class A voting shares were worth more than class B non-voting shares, but he disagreed with both parties as to the dollar value, although his honor's price was closer to that of the IRS: class A, $215,539 per share; class B, $3,417 per share.

The judge claimed that if the company ever considered merging—selling some or all its assets, or going public—only the holders of voting shares could make the decisions and that therefore those shares were worth more. Moreover, if the company were to remain private, only voting share-holders were in a position to make company decisions. It would be possible, said the judge, for Richard's block of shares to become the largest block because the brothers' and sister's shares would pass on to their children and no single shareholder would own more than eighteen shares.

The judge's ruling meant that the estate owed less than the IRS demanded (some $17.6 million), although the precise amount had not yet been calculated since the two parties must take the judge's reasoning and apply it to the arithmetic of the case and arrive at a figure acceptable to the judge.

Added to the taxes was a penalty of $7,057,554 because the payment offered by the estate was considerably different from what the IRS demanded. However, Judge Jacobs rejected the penalty because, he said, the estate had calculated its obligations in good faith, relying upon the best advice from tax experts, including Morgan Stanley and Company.[5]

Since 1994, Don, Gay, Scott, and grandson Ted have shared the responsibilities of chairman of the board because Jack officially retired.[6] Company

President Gordon Smith was followed in that office by Steve Beebe. With all those changes, one might wonder whether Jack Simplot is still actively interested in the affairs of the company. One might as well ask the rhetorical question, "Is the pope Catholic?"

Simplot is vitally interested in every aspect of the operation of his "rig." Ask him about any one of its components and as he answers, that particular component inspires impassioned responses. Charles J. V. Murphy caught the essential Simplot in his *Fortune* magazine story of 1968:

> *Givin' up what I've built would be the same as givin' up part of myself.*[7]

This is not to say that if an element of his outfit proves undesirable or unprofitable he will not close it out; he will: the company is no longer in the cheese-milk business, although his transportation unit still contracts to haul milk. Nor is it to say that his counsel is not available to the stockholders: it is, and they listen. The passion for his outfit boils beneath the surface, but age has prompted him to put a safety gauge on it.

There is, for instance, the recent purchase of the largest privately owned ranch in the United States, the ZX Ranch of central Oregon. In talking about it, Jack can contain himself . . . but just barely:

> *It's 136 miles long and sixty-five miles wide. It's a big area! You can't believe it 'till you see it.*[8]

The ranch includes 35,000 acres of peat, and with the ranch go vast range rights, that is, the right to run cattle on the public domain. Simplot's holdings are so vast that he is unquestionably the largest private landowner in the state and one of the largest in the American West. He says he has 400,000 deeded acres, and when Vice President Fred Zerza was consulted, the following breakdown was given:

Simplot personally (through his trust) has 101,700 deeded acres and holds leases on another 1,839,000 acres. That includes eleven different properties (farms and, primarily, ranches). The Simplot Company and other Simplot family members have 227,770 deeded acres and leases on another 1,051,300 acres. Included are fifty-four farms and ranches. Overall, that's 329,470 deeded and 2,890,300 leased acres. J. R. is responsible for the acquisition of virtually all the acreage. . . . The leases are primarily BLM but include some U.S. Forest Service and State (mainly Idaho) leases. The sixty-five properties included in the numbers above are located in Southern Idaho (Elmore, Owyhee, Payette, and Cassia counties); Eastern Washington (Franklin and Walla Walla counties); Oregon (Lake and Umatilla counties) and there are ranches (one each) in Northern Utah, Northern Nevada, and Northern California. Incidentally, about 1.3 million of J. R.'s 1.8 million leased acres are for the ZX Ranch in Oregon.[9]

There is also the expansion of his Grand View, Idaho, feedlot, which has now absorbed all the livestock from Caldwell, making it the largest feedlot in the United States. Its new annual capacity represents a thirty-six percent increase, from 330,000 head to

450,000. Consistent with Simplot's economies of production strategies, the beef from the feedlot will be processed at an Iowa Beef (IBP Inc.) plant close to nearby Kuna, Idaho. The Grand View location is also strategically located within about twenty miles of a newly expanded and modernized grain terminal near Mountain Home, Idaho. A story in the *Idaho Statesman* of March 9, 1999, makes clear the fact that this is an operation on an unprecedented scale: a Union Pacific locomotive will pull up to 126 hopper cars of grains of various kinds into the $5 million facility, each car unloading its contents in seven minutes while proceeding around a 7,400-foot oval terminating back at the main line. The entire train will be unloaded in fifteen hours. Simplot's own trucks will then transport the grain to the facility at Grand View. Company spokesman Fred Zerza is quoted as saying, "Union Pacific can ship grain to us at better rates than they could with smaller numbers of cars. The terminal also improves the ability of our feedlot to compete with feedlots closer to sources of grain in the Midwest."[10]

With between 40,000 and 50,000 head of cows producing calves, feedlots in Grand View, Idaho, and Pasco, Washington, reliable sources of, and transportation for, grain, and easy and quick access to slaughterhouses, Jack Simplot has created a model of production economies with no middle men anywhere along the line. He has to buy some feeders, for he cannot produce enough beef animals to fill his stockyards, but that problem may resolve itself in the future.

Simplot thinks globally and wants a ranch in

Australia, where he now has eleven big plants, including a bakery. He explains the situation this way:

> *We gotta start looking and showing . . . . I can take you to Maine, and I can take you to Canada. It'd take a week to show you what we've got. We got 'em, and they're beautiful. I've got some of the nicest spots on earth. Biggest plants and the most beautiful country! And you can see those plants up there on that [Canadian] prairie . . . hundred miles and you'll see a big tower . . . It'll be our fertilizer operation. And we've got a hundred and some of 'em. Then you go to Australia. That's another one.*
>
> *We do everything! Eleven BIG plants in Australia. These plants are big! We have a bakery. I was there at four or five in the morning, and there were seventy-five trucks backed up against that bakery, and the bakery's so big you can't believe it . . . several stories high and right in the middle of town. And that's just one of them. We've got the biggest potato plant in the world . . . . And we're big in tomatoes . . . make every kind of paste and sauce, everything.*
>
> *. . .We market it! Hundreds of labels! Canned and frozen products! It's big.*[11]

But it is clear that he wants a ranch down under:

> *I'm going to buy a million acres, irrigate it, grow potatoes . . .* [and] *ship 'em north.*

North, of course, suggesting China, and Simplot may be right that french fries can compete with rice, judging by the success McDonald's has had.[12]

There is considerable food for thought here: Simplot produces that as well as food for the table. But such production challenges some of his convictions about the future, as we shall see.

Chapter Twelve Notes

1. The preceding analysis of the Simplot empire is from Bob Eure's "Ridin' High with J. R. Simplot," which appeared in the *Sunday Oregonian* of June 20, 1996.

2. pp. 6-7, "Wildest Billionaire in the West," November 27, 1995, *Fortune.*

3. The writer is Andrew Serwer ("Wildest Billionaire in the West," 8-9). Micron did not move to Lehi; it did not have to, for the powers of state government acceded to the wishes of its wealthiest citizen. While it is true that an engineering school at Boise State University is a great convenience for the local electronics firms, it is also true that an accredited engineering program of first magnitude was already in place at Idaho's land grant institution, the University of Idaho at Moscow. The episode is part of a continuing paradigmatic shift in American education in which students demand and receive instruction where it is most convenient for them. Once upon a time students gravitated to centers of instruction (where programs, facilities, and professors were located) and accommodated themselves to that environment, regardless of travel time, travel expense, and the costs of living away from home. When contemporary student demand for instruction that is located near home is buttressed by industry's pleas, which seem to be ultimately reducible to arguments based on convenience, politicians listen while college administrators murmur that "modern educational delivery systems must be designed to meet the students' needs where the students are" and that "distance learning is the tidal wave of the future," forgetting, as administrators are wont to do, that the transmission and absorption of information has never been and will never be the same as getting an education.

4. 11-18-98m tape 2, side A.

5. April 4, 1999.

6 Eure, "Ridin' High with J. R. Simplot," *Sunday Oregonian*, June 30, 1996.

7. "Jack Simplot and His Private Conglomerate," August, 1968, 172.

8 JRS, 4-8-99, tape 1, side A.

9. e-mail, 25 Feb 2000.

10 Paul Beebe, byline. It should be noted that Simplot has his own slaughterhouse in Nampa, Idaho, where Holstein cattle are fattened so as to produce highly marbled meat, which is then shipped to Japan. 135

11. JRS, 10-20-98, tape 1, side B. Jack thinks and talks in superlatives; there is no type font that can convey the excitement and passion that his rich voice and his animated features convey. It is probably a good thing that his energies do not take a religious bent, for he could likely separate a great many true believers from their fortunes and teach some of the amateur televangelists a thing or two.

12. quoted in Eure, "Ridin' High with J. R. Simplot," *Sunday Oregonian*, June 30, 1996.

Chapter Thirteen

Sands at ninety[1]

In order to sharpen our awareness of a contemporary disingenuousness about life, about the use of natural resources, about the production of goods, and about the satisfaction of wants and necessities, the following thoughts are offered.

To some, Jack Simplot is the incarnation of the corporate farmer or worse yet the *corporation* . . . big, efficient, and willing to sacrifice anything for profit. Such critics are unwilling—or unable—to grant that he worked his way through the chairs to his present position, that he was a small farmer, that he had been a small potato sorter and shipper. If he has succeeded in increasing the yield of his potato fields by a significant arithmetic factor, the same technology is available to all farmers. If the processes of production and consumption create waste and fallout, so does life itself, as Willa Cather, one of our finest writers, makes abundantly clear in *My Ántonia* when the narrator describes winter in a small midwestern town: "The growing piles of ashes and cinders in the back yards were the only evidence that the wasteful, consuming processes of life went on at all."[2] "Growing piles of ashes and cinders": life *is* wasteful and consuming. Procreation generates needs. Those needs must be met, if the species is to fulfill its evolutionary role and occupy its biological niche.

Some observers have looked at primitive peoples and have concluded, perhaps prematurely, that such peoples lived in a world in which homeostasis prevailed. That is, these observers believed that the relationships among all life forms and the environment were such that the system *then* was in perfect harmony and balance. But that may well be a sentimentalist's view of things. It is unlikely that any one who scrutinizes human culture carefully will find societies in which warfare, slavery, and economic exploitation, to identify only a few examples of imbalance, did not flourish at some time or other.

Examination of the globe continent by continent, pole to pole, and meridian by meridian shows the exploiter and the exploited, the enslaver and the enslaved. Even the paradise of the South Pacific revealed to Herman Melville a sordid underside when in the jewel of the Marquesas Islands he discovered the native fondness for "long pig," *puarkee* in their dialect; that is, barbecued human beings. In the contrasting world views of John Calvin, on the one hand, and Jean Jacques Rousseau, on the other, Calvin seems much more attuned to the realities of human existence. If his emphasis on the depraved or fallen nature of the species is accurate to the slightest degree, then those flaws are universally distributed throughout the species. They are human flaws. To do a violent injustice to Robert Louis Stevenson, the failings are found in Little Indian Sioux or Crow/Little Frosty Eskimo/Little Turk or Japanee . . . and in the heart of Africa and anywhere else one might look, including Iceland and Greece where democracy has dwelled a long time.

It is a world, in short, where competition is keen and where the least kind of technological advance gives great advantage over a competitor who has only ritual and belief, prayer and propitiation. It is a world that Jack Simplot has characterized time after time as rough and tough, a world described most accurately by Charles Darwin or his popularizers . . . those who survive are the ones fittest to survive, a neatly circular assertion. But there should be no doubt that Jack is a philosophical materialist. His own words on the subject are clear and unequivocal:

> *I know how I got here, and I know . . . where I'm going. I haven't got any worries, and I'm not trying to get anybody into heaven 'cause I don't believe in it. . .*[3] *I'm too much of a facts man, and . . . when they start tellin' me that Christ was born of a virgin . . . I say there's no way.* [It's a] *bunch of hocus pocus. And I've been that way all my life. Churches are beyond me. I just never criticized them.*[4]

It is consistent with his philosophical materialism that Jack should be Darwinian in both his understanding of biology and his understanding of the way society works. To put that slightly differently, he believes in social and biological Darwinism: the fittest survive because the great mechanism of the world, a kind of cream separator, brings to the top those whose struggles to get there are in harmony with the operations of the centrifuge. Natural selection may take a long time, but it always works. There is nothing easy about the process, either sociologically or biologically. . . it's a rough, tough world out there. Again, it is instructive to hear his own voice. What does he think of the push by some to teach creationism instead of evolution in school?

> *They know where we come from. Go ask anybody! The only way we could get here* [is] *through evolution. There's no other . . . way in the world. And if you don't believe it, you go down there and look at these bones they're diggin' up . . . those old dinosaurs. They got big. They weighed forty tons, those babies.*[5] *This old earth is something else. It's been kicked around and tumbled . . . look at the rocks, look at those bones! They're real. They were a livin' animal, probably fifty million years ago . . . . This thing's been here a long time, and you just don't know where the hell it came from. But you look at these stars at night, and you say, "My God, it's a massive, massive, massive universe." And it startles you; it just really startles you. And then you take Halley's Comet . . . it gets around here every seventy-five years. You say to yourself, "Fella, how big is this thing,*

and does it go on forever? Where does it stop? And what's beyond the stop?[6]

"What's beyond the stop?" is as neat a way to put the great cosmological enigma as anyone has ever phrased that question. What, indeed, is beyond the stop? But as to the here and now, there are plenty of questions and more than a few answers.

There is, for instance, the question of health and longevity. Jack likes to say that he has never been sick a day in his life, never had a headache and so on. A couple of broken legs in the forties (1940 and 1947)—each leg was broken once—don't count as sickness. They were more like a mechanical breakdown, and he didn't miss a day in the office. Some broken ribs from a horseback incident was an accident. Both hips were replaced (1990 and 1995); that put an end to his horseback riding and skiing. And in 1998 an attack of sciatica that left him experiencing shocks when he bent over and straightened up, well, that was fixed surgically.[7]

It was not so much sickness as it was a mechanical problem. Also in this decade he underwent a prostate procedure. But the big medical problem of this decade was open heart surgery on August 5, 1999, during which five blockages were corrected in a four-hour operation. He made a good recovery, for he had taken good care of himself, remarking once that he had to *stay* in shape because at his age it was too hard to *get* in shape. A story in the *Idaho Statesman* quoted Fred Zerza as saying that Simplot had often said publicly that he would buy parts whenever necessary, for he plans to stay around as long as possible.[8]

Then there is the matter of Jack Simplot's philanthropy, no insignificant item in any inventory of the differences this man, with his company, has made in Idaho, primarily, but including any part of the globe where the company operates. Speaking of Jack's public image as a tightwad, television personality and newsman Sal Celeski asked Jack, "Are you tight?" Simplot responded, "I'm not the loosest guy in the world."[9] The viewer's attention was directed to the first pair of reading glasses that Simplot had bought in 1951, and he was still using them.

His company's sponsorship of the annual Simplot Games in Pocatello has been mentioned as has his sixty-year-long connection with Albertson College of Idaho as both trustee and chairman of the board of trustees. His generosity to the institution may not be so well known: for most of the last forty years it has been his principal cause, with his contributions amounting to something in excess of $5 million.[10] His previously cited sponsorship of the anti-tobacco speaker and his sponsoring of traffic safety promoter Glenn H. "Safety" Davis should be mentioned. There is also his sponsorship of the Boise Philharmonic, including his gift of start-up money, his assistance to hospitals and the YWCA, and his generosity to Booth Memorial Hospital, which specializes in help for unwed mothers. "And one of the little known secrets was that he gave Bogus Basin, (the site of a popular public ski resort), to the City of Boise. Just two years ago they did a great big article in the *Statesman*, and it was never mentioned . . . ."[11]

How much he has given to assist individuals, like The Rev. E. Rohn, like students in graduate and professional school, like relatives down on their luck, is a matter of conjecture. Unlike the sanctimonious Rockefeller, who apparently really believed that he was God's bursar and what he was disbursing carried with it the possibility of eternal damnation if it were misused, Jack has given of his largess with zest and with few regrets.

There is also the matter of Jack's unitarianism, not the Unitarian-Universalist denomination, but another speculative and philosophical notion. It bears examination because the idea holds certain implications that seem at first glance quite uncharacteristic of this man.

Esther Becker Simplot was asked what she thinks historians 200 years from now will say about her husband Jack:

> *I think he'll go down as one of the real . . . what should I say? . . . entrepreneur-geniuses of this century. There are a number of them; I couldn't name them all . . . . But his story is such a basic . . . one, and yet he did it with so little education. And this happened, I think, with Ford and many other of the entrepreneurs . . . of that time. He's just one of the more unusual ones. I think* [that] *like Rockefeller and Ford he chose to keep the company private for a period of time, and he still wants it to be private. So he's a little unique there perhaps—*

kind of works to build a dynasty, very interested in keeping it for his posterity. But I think it's a great mind, a great intuitiveness. . . . He has a lot of knowledge. I'm always amazed at the knowledge he has about fertilizers and chemistry. And I took chemistry in high school and college, and I don't remember 1/100th of what he knows and what he's learned through life's experiences. So he's in a sense more educated about many things than I am. He's really learned through doing, and missing, and trying again and making a success of his life in the business world. So I think he'll stand out for a long, long time.

You know, his focus and his energy are just something to behold. He has so much energy that I think for the first twenty years that I was married to him I was in a continuous state of exhaustion trying to keep up with him. And I'm not lying. He sleeps three or four hours a night; everybody knows that. Then he would think, and he would visualize, and he would plan what he was going to do either ten years ahead or the next day. And that's when he would get some of his greatest ideas, because he'd had his sleep, and he would just lie there, and it was quiet, and he'd just think. And then he would be up at 5:30 and off on his horses or off to look at a ranch, or whatever he had to do that day. The energy is incredible, and I find this is apparently true of many entrepreneurs and men of his stature. But I was a little bit glad when he got to be eighty so that he slowed down just a little bit, so that maybe I had a chance to keep up with him.[12]

After living through the best and the worst of the twentieth century, Jack Simplot has a challenging view of the twenty-first:

I think in this next hundred years it'll boil down to one language, one money, and one president . . . in the next hundred years. . . . I think we've got to stop the killing. I think we've got it stopped. But you know in my lifetime I don't know how many millions of people we've slaughtered. I mean millions! With the Stalins and the Nazis and . . . you know you go on and on and on. We [have to] *stop the killing and try to bring education forward with enough new equipment like these . . . computers. . . . Awesome, the possiblities of the world. . . .*

I don't know how far I can get, but I'm leavin' whatever I've got—could be a billion dollars, I hope. And I'm gonna leave it for this museum and try to fly people in here from all over the world and let 'em see: here's how we got here, and this is the machinery that did it, and show 'em a picture that might create unity throughout the world. And I think if we don't get it under one head you're gonna get two, and when you get two you're apt to be back fightin'. And there's no reason for it.

The killin's stopped pretty well. We'll have to regulate the population, naturally, but we'll

> *build a world that works. And it works by the vote of the people. And how far we can go with it, only time will tell because there's only this one planet. You start thinking' about other planets, and I think it took seven years to get that little tractor down on Mars—took seven years to get it there, for God's sakes! . . . . The future's not ours to see, but I think America's going to lead the world in a democracy, and we've got to get a world-wide currency, and we've got to get a world-wide police force, and we've got to run the universe.*[13]

On the subject of an international language to go along with his ideas about universal democracy, he affirms that English "is the best one [language] and it's been tried and it's working. And it's going to take time and generations, but I think we've got the battle [won]."[14]

In what might appear an abrupt about face, Simplot seems to push aside *laissez-faire* capitalism and become an advocate of what John D. Rockefeller had discovered in his struggles against destructive competition in the oil business after the Civil War. Simplot's unitary, one world, one police force, one language philosophy may to be the next stage in the processes of the evolution of business.

This sober affirmation may well indicate the line of cleavage between Simplot and those who profess, or claim to profess, what they think Adam Smith advocated in the eighteenth century, *laissez-faire, laissez-*

passer. Of the various elements at work here to control competition, one, the favorite of John D. Rockefeller, Sr., is noteworthy: the formation of combines from erstwhile competitors. Edward Bellamy's noted assessment of this late 19th century phenomenon is almost prophetic in light of today's fevered formation of combines as corporation swallows corporation, creating fewer and fewer but bigger and bigger organizations. *Looking Backward* (1888) anticipates this frenzy with its consequence of the death of competition.

John D. Rockefeller, Sr., chuckled at "academic enthusiasts" and scorned the textbook evocation of free markets inspired by Adam Smith, preferring instead a world of economic cooperation.[15] It would appear that Jack Simplot's endorsement of the principles of evolution can accommodate both the principle of natural selection and the formation of monopolies. After all, those creatures that survive are those most fit to survive, and if nature's great cream separator brings to the top those creations that result from cooperation, their triumph is no less secure.[16]

It may be that Jack Simplot recognizes trends and sees no way of countering them. The future will take its own shape regardless of attempts to control it. If combines are going to be formed, he may feel powerless to stop the process. It would be easy to say that his early exposure to Presbyterian notions absorbed from John Calvin made predestinarianism inevitable. And it is possible.

On the subject of religion, one of the three remaining subjects on which to shed some light (if not a glare) in this concluding chapter. In *King of the Hill* Jack says that he has his own religion and that "We're all working for the same guy," that we need something to tie to. This is followed by his favorite existential theme that "this is pretty good right here, and I plan to stay as long as I can." He cannot worry about the hereafter, if there is one.

In the same TV feature, he says, "There's nothing to this money" a claim that comes easier for the wealthy than for the impecunious. He follows this with the observation that what matters is the chase, the fun of it.[17]

> *I know I'm gonna keep my Micron* [stock]. *Course, I'm gamblin', and I don't mind puttin' my money down and bettin' it. Maybe I'll lose it, but if I do, nobody's hurt but me.*

Is Jack Simplot a venture capitalist or a gambler?

> *Well . . . both. I'm a venture capitalist.*[18]

As to his notion of business ethics, Simplot says that he has taken advantage of everything he could, but that he has never "frauded" anybody. He follows this comment with a one sentence dismissal of socialism and devotes equal time to communism:

> *Socialism can't work, and communism is slavery.*

Additional insights from the *King of the Hill*

documentary allow that he may be one of the five richest people in the United States, that his is one of the largest family-owned corporations of its kind in the world, that he is one of the largest potato processors in the world, that he inherited no money, and that he may be the last self-made billionaire.[19] Whatever discounting must be made in the interests of truth, Jack Simplot has come a long way since moving onto the Minidoka Project in 1910.

What memories are his. . . getting to know Bing Crosby, for they had adjoining ranches in Nevada, and forming a close friendship with Lowell Thomas, skiing with him and traveling around the world with him on two different occasions. But of all the days of his life, the one most memorable . . . . But we let him tell it:

> *The day of my life that I can remember best was the time we* [Nelson Rockefeller and JRS] *drove down that dam twenty miles. And it was at the tail end of the season, and there was water back maybe a quarter of a mile. . . . And the birds! Millions of parrots living off that dam.*[20]

What a sight it must have been and what an experience with living color to store away in the mind.

Chapter Thirteen Notes

1. When Walt Whitman was seventy years of age, he put together "annexes" to the collection of his verse *Leaves of Grass*, and because in some respects Walt Whitman and Jack Simplot share ideas (in others they are radically dissimilar), this chapter takes its name from the title Whitman gave to the first collection of poems added to his major work. He called it "First Annex: Sands at Seventy." It was, of course, an appropriate recognition that the sands in Whitman's hourglass were running out. At ninety, Jack gave up some of the activities in which he had delighted, and one can be sure that the sand remaining in his hourglass is that high grade silica from his Nevada sand deposit whose mining and refining contribute some $10 million annually to the company revenues.

2. (Boston: Houghton Mifflin Company, 1949) 144.

3. JRS, 9-24-98, tape 4, side A.

4. JRS, 11-18-98, tape 2, side A. Jack's inability to accept the "hocus pocus" of Christianity or any other revealed religion did not stop him from extending kindness to people like Rev. E. Rohn. Jack tells it this way: "Rev. Rohn came to me, and if I haven't told you this story, it's a good one, and I was out there working [in the box factory in Caldwell] and he came to me and he said, 'Jack, I was in my prayin' power last night and got it direct from the old man that I was to look after you and your dad. Get you on the right side of the fence.' And I never went to his church. But he would come and see me, oh, once or twice a month. And he'd telephone me. And he did it fifty years! I knew him, I never went to his church, [Pentecostal Tabernacle, 208 S. 6th] but he'd come over here when I lived in Caldwell, and he would [visit] my dad when he died [in 1974]. And he called me a thousand times . . . easy. Maybe more. Every week or so he'd call me to see how I was. And he came to me one time and he said, 'I want to go to Pocatello.' There was another preacher down there he wanted to see, so I said 'All right.' I'd moved to Boise and I said, 'You keep track of my pilot. . . Kilbourne' and the next time I was going to Pocatello—I was building my plant down there—well, I got ready to go and there he was sittin' in the front seat of the airplane, and we started to Pocatello. And we got around Mountain Home, and it got rough as hell, and he got sick. And I said to him, 'Now pray a little, Reverend—God can handle a little deal like that!' And he came up and said, 'I gotta get off, I gotta.' So I stopped at Jerome and let him off, and I gave him $40—two $20 bills. I remember that. And I said, 'I don't know how you're gonna get to town, but you'll have to bum a ride . . . . ' There wasn't anybody out there at the airport. But he got a ride to Pocatello and saw his partner. He got it in his head it was his duty [to look after] me." Jack speculates that Rev. Rohn built an expensive home with tax free money and says, " I thought someday I'd hire somebody to check that out and see how much taxes Rev. Rohn paid in his lifetime . But I don't care . . . . Hell, I never had an inch of religion . . . . Still, [religion is] the cause of this [Balkan] war. They just want to kick all the

Muslims out of the country . . .' cause the Muslims are holding the land, and they want it . . . . But we'll get that stopped." 9-16-98, tape 1, side A.

5. ibid.

6. ibid.

7. When he was asked whether he had high blood pressure or headaches, he replied: "No, I never had a headache . . . . I never had any aches other than the time I had this back operation . . . . My sciatic nerve . . . they just knock you down once in a while . . . and I couldn't get comfortable in bed. I mean it was terrible: you bend over, you know, and straighten up and you get some shocks. Anyway, I went in [to the hospital] and ten minutes after the operation, I said, "Hell, I'm gonna see if I can stand up." I got out of bed and stood up and didn't have an ache or a pain and I said to my wife,"Let's get the hell out of here." 9-24-98, tape 3, side A. He later said that he had spent only one night in the hospital, so his departure may have been the day after the surgery.

8. August 5, 1999.

9. *King of the Hill.*

10. ibid.

11. EBS, 2-9-00, tape1, side A.

12. ibid.

13. JRS, 9-24-98, tape 4, side A.

14. ibid.

15. Ron Chernow presents these ideas on page 148 and page xx "(Prelude") of *Titan: The Life of John D. Rockefeller, Sr.* (New York: Random House, 1998).

16. In connection with his notions about one government, one police force, and so on Jack has given thought to the United Nations and to other organizations which seem to meet his ideas about social evolution. The present organization clearly evolved from the earlier ineffective League of Nations, and the World Trade Organization and the World Health Organization seem also to indicate a broadening acceptance of the fact that there is only one, single, unitary planet earth.

17. *King of the Hill.*

18. JRS, 11-18-98, tape 2, side A.

19. *King of the Hill.*

20. JRS, 2-14-2000, tape 1, side A.

Chapter Fourteen

Afterword

As the hourglass dominating the creation of this book signals conclusion and its sands cascade to their final resting place, we take not a backward glance over roads reader and writer have taken together but a look ahead. It is appropriate to do so, because that's the way Jack's head was nearly always turned.

It has been a dream of his for some time to create a museum of agricultural artifacts, not just a repository of machinery but a first-class teaching and learning environment.

> *You start thinking about* [interplanetary exploration] *and you say, "Well . . . it's impossible. Have they got air* [on other planets]*? Have they got water? . . . . You look out at that mass of stars and the Milky Way and you say to yourself, "My God, it's so big and so complicated . . . ." And my thinking is we'd better*

polish this old world we got. We've got a gorgeous place for humanity to thrive and live. We can feed a lot of people . . . . We can build a world we're proud of and support whatever millions of people we want, and build a society, a human society, on this earth that we can be awfully proud of.

I don't know . . . . It's just an old man's thinking, but you know, I think with a big museum and three or four of those big airplanes running . . . you know, you can fly from here to Timbuktu without stopping. When you load them up, two or three or four hundred kids on these big airplanes and bring them in here and give them a week to study and to look and see how far we've come. And here's the machinery that got us here. And we can see if we can't steer the world in the right direction to peace and prosperity . . . . It can be done through a democracy. . . . What I'm trying to think about is bigger than anybody's got today . . . . I'll get a couple of these big jets and bring people from all over the world in here to look at this museum and to get a picture of what a democracy does. And sell the world on democracy . . . . In this next hundred years, I think it will boil down to one language, one money, and one president. . . . I don't know how far I can get, but I'm leaving whatever I've got—could be a billion dollars, I hope. Today it's over six hundred-seven hundred million. And I'm going to leave this for the . . . museum.[1] *If I have enough money, I'm going to build a big five hundred or six hundred-room hotel . . .six to seven hundred kids a day for a week . . . . I don't know. Maybe I'll never get it done, but I've had it in mind for a long time, and I've started to pick up a lot of junk . . . you can see the machines, you can walk around them, you can use them, you can sit down, and we'll have a movie for everything and try to explain it and make an educational leap that the world will envy.*[2]

Finally, what happens when John Richard Simplot can't get the necessary replacement parts to keep on "hanging on"? What legacy will he leave behind? His daughter, Gay, speculated on how historians 200 years from now will view her father:

Well, if they didn't really know him, they'd look back . . . saying he was an entrepreneur. Others [see] *a person that backed his word with actions, believed in what he was doing, and didn't hesitate to put every resource he had behind it.*

Personally, I think of him as being a genuine person. He loves people; he wants to see them succeed. He wants to succeed himself, but he wants to see people around him succeed. He's very down to earth; when you talk to him you feel he's really interested in what you're doing, what you see in the future, what you think. . . . His success in life was to be able to pick people he could trust and who could believe in his visions and execute them. . ."[3]

Hers is an affirmative perception, not only of her father but also of those believing in and helping realize the visions of Jack Simplot who, for over ninety years, has heard America singing.

Afterword Notes

1. JRS, 14-2-2000, tape 1, side A.

2. JRS, 11-18-98, tape 2, side A. On May 19 Jack talked at somewhat greater length on this subject, and part of that conversation is included here so that the curious reader may study a slightly fuller statement of this notion. He was asked: In view of your convictions about one world, one currency, one language, one kind of government, do you think the United Nations is a step in the evolution of a world union? He replied: "Well, naturally. They'll all have to be in step, but how you going to keep them regulated without it? The first thing you know we'll be fighting again. . . . I think we've done all the killing we're going to kill. People won't put up with it any more. . . . I've got an imagination, and it's only that [but] I'm gonna build a museum . . . and I'm gonna put a billion dollars in it. And I want to try to mix the world up . . .get me a couple of these big airplanes, and I'll bring in kids from all over the world and let 'em see: Here's America! Here's the machinery that got us here! The human . . . [well] there's no hocus pocus [divine intervention] out there [so] the human's got to get back to facts."

When asked if he thought in addition to the United Nations the World Health Organization and the World Trade Organization were steps in the evolution of a unified world, he responded: "That's just an old farmer's idea, and it's mine, and I think it'll happen . . . because it's a necessity. [We've] got to have the [approval] of the people, [and when we do] we can run this world like we want to, and if [we] don't [we'll] overpopulate . . . and we'll get back to where we can't feed 'em and [we] can't do this and [we] can't do that. So you have to put some discipline some place. . . . It's something we all have to start thinking about. We are all humans, and you can mix 'em up any way you want to mix them, and they'll cross, and they're all on the same tree. . . . We're humans, and we're supposed to be smart, and you know we're not goin' anywhere . . . very soon. [How many years did it take]. . . to get that little tractor on Mars?"

3. GCS, 1-26-2000, tape 1, side A.

The Author

Dr. Louie W. Attebery is an authority on American folklore. He is former chairman of the Department of English at Albertson College of Idaho in Caldwell, Idaho. He was a member of the first executive council of the Western Literature Association. He has given numerous talks on American and Western folklore and was folklife consultant for the 1974 World's Fair in Spokane, Washington. He has written numerous articles for regional and national publications. Dr. Attebery is a former editor of *Northwest Folklore* and is a contributor to the *Encyclopedia of American Folklore* He has written several books, and edited *Idaho Folklife: Homesteads to Headstones*.

Bibliography

Sources consulted

Abbreviations

Two discrete audio-taped interview series appear frequently throughout this study, one undertaken at the behest of the J. R. Simplot Company and conducted by Steve Richardson, the other conducted by the author of this book and undertaken with the permission of the principals being interviewed. The book is thus an amalgam of oral history, with the kind of immediacy that research technique provides, and traditional research in secondary sources.

CHP—J. R. Simplot Company History Project

DJS, EBS, GCS, JRS, RRS, SRS—Initials of family members and a former family member interviewed by the author, namely, Don John Simplot, Esther Becker Simplot, Gay Corrine Simplot, John Richard Simplot, Ruby Rosevear Shipp, and Scott Robert Simplot.

Bibliography

Adjutant General of the State of Oregon. *Twenty-first Biennial Report, 1927-1928.*

Allen, Frederick Lewis. *Only Yesterday.* New York: Bantam Books, 1931.

Arrington, Leonard. "Irrigation in the Snake River Valley: An Historical Overview." *Idaho Yesterdays*. Spring-Summer, Vol. 30, No. 1-2, 1986.

Attebery, Louie W. "From Littoral to Lateral." *Idaho Yesterdays*. Spring-Summer, Vol. 30, No. 1-2, 1986.

Bailey, Allen M. "Work Key Word in Simplot Story." *Idaho State Journal.* August 14, 1968.

Beebe, Paul. "Simplot Unveils Huge Grain Terminal." *Idaho Statesman*, April 4, 1999.

Bunderson, Hal. *Idaho Entrepreneurs*. Boise: Boise State University, 1992.

Cather, Willa. *My Ántonia.* Boston: Houghton Mifflin Company, 1949.

Chernow, Ron. *Titan: The Life of John D. Rockefeller, Sr.* New York: Random House, 1998.

Davis, James W. *Aristocrat in Burlap: A History of the Potato in Idaho*. The Idaho Potato Commission. n.p. 1992.

Declo History Committee. *Declo- My Town My People*. Burley, Idaho: The Burley Reminder, Inc., 1974.

Eure, Bob. "Ridin' High with J. R. Simplot," *The Sunday Oregonian*. June 30, 1996.

Gilder, George. *The Spirit of Enterprise.* New York: Simon and Schuster, 1984.

Hall, William W., Jr. *The Small College Talks Back: An Intimate Appraisal.* New York: Richard R. Smith, 1951.

Hamsun, Knut. *Growth of the Soil*. trans. by W. W. Worster. New York: The Modern Library, 1921.

James Herriot's Yorkshire. New York: St. Martin's Press, 1979.

Hill, Jim Dan. *The Minute Man in Peace and War: A History of the National Guard.* Harrisburg, Pennsylvania: The Stackpole Company,1964.

Jenning, Steve. "The Potato Billionaire." *Northwest, The Oregonian's Sunday Magazine*. October 20, 1985.

King of the Hill, Sal Celeski, host, produced by KTVB News and Special Affairs, May 1982.

Kirstner, Cherie. "Springfield, Oregon, School," e-mail,1/27/99.

Lowitt, Richard. "Irrigation Agriculture in Idaho as Seen by Henry A. Wallace in 1909." *Idaho Yesterdays*. Vol. 35, No. 1, Spring 1991.

Lucas, Anthony. J. *Big Trouble*. New York: Simon and Schuster, 1997.

Martin, Richard. "Alexander Simplot—Artist." *The Palimpsest* 17. January 1965.

McCrum, Robert, William Cran, and Robert MacNeil. *The Story of English*. New York: Penguin Books, 1986.

Moulton, Kristen. "J. R. Simplot: The Man and the Empire," *The Idaho Statesman*, April 11, 1999.

Murphy, Charles J. V. "Jack Simplot and His Private Conglomerate." *Fortune*, August 1968.

Neuberger, Richard L. "Idaho's Fantastic Millionaire." *Saturday Evening Post*, June 19, 1948.

Origins of the J. R. Simplot Company: Boise, 1997.

Parnell, Dusty. "Simplot on Mend from Bypass Surgery," *Idaho Press-Tribune*, August 6, 1999.

Riesman, David. *The Lonely Crowd: A Study of the Changing American Character*. Abridged Edition with a New Foreword. New Haven & London: Yale University Press, 1961.

Ringle, William M. "Tax Fight Gives Look at Simplot Money," *Idaho Statesman*, April 4, 1999.

Rosholt, John. "Irrigation and Politics." *Idaho Yesterdays*. Spring-Summer, Vol. 30, No. 1-2, 1986.

Serwer, Andrew E. "Wildest Billionaire in the West." *Fortune*, November 27, 1995.

Simkins, Karen. *A Chronology of the J. R. Simplot Company*. Boise: J. R. Simplot Company, 1993.

"Simplot Faces Tax Charge." *Idaho State Journal*, May 4, 1977.

Waksman, Selman A. *The Conquest of Tuberculosis*. Berkeley and Los Angeles: University of California Press, 1964.

Wilbur, Richard. "Potato." *The Beautiful Changes and Other Poems.* New York: Harcourt, Brace and World, 1947.

Woodhouse, Michael V. "Potato Sorting," e-mail, 1/27/99.

Zerza, Fred. "Simplot Deeded Acres," e-mail, 1/25/00.

Index

46th Iowa Volunteers 4

A

Aberdeen 136
Afton, Wyoming 194
Albion Normal 77
Tom Alexander 76
Frederick Lewis Allen 59
American Falls, Idaho 143
Anaconda Company 141
Anaconda, Montana 141
Steve Appleton 204
Arid Club 204
Asbury Road 6
Auburn, California 137

B

Bakersfield, California 136
John Basabe 92, 196
Tom Basabe 196
Bayard, Nebraska 143
Steve Beebe 92, 167
Dave Bennnett 22
Besancón, France 2
Blackfoot, Idaho 137
Bogus Basin 222
Boise Cascade 203
Boise Philharmonic 222
Boise State University 205
Boise, Idaho xix, 80, 113, 133, 151, 158, 203
Mary Ellen Bonson 6
Mary Spensley Bonson 5
Priscilla Bonson 6
Richard Bonson 4, 7, 97
Robert Bonson 4, 8, 9
Booth Memorial Hospital 222
Catherine Bourquin 2
John Braden 33
Dorothy Bradley 10
Brandon, Manitoba, Canada 143, 193
Bruneau Sheep Company 94
Buffalo Bill Cody 203
Buhl, Idaho 136
Burbank Corporation 87
Burbank, California 84, 85
Burley, Idaho 21, 35, 36, 76, 78, 79, 101, 129, 136, 147, 150, 151, 166
Jane Burton 5, 6
Butte, Montana 68

C

Cal-Ida Lumber Company 130, 154, 194
Caldwell Feeders 94
Caldwell Lumber Company 94, 136
Caldwell, Idaho 20, 80, 86, 93, 94, 113, 128, 136, 137, 147, 151, 152, 196, 212
Camp Jackson, Oregon 64
Carberry, Canada 142
Carey Act 19, 20, 114
Carnation Foods Company 142, 147
Catfish Creek 8
Willa Cather 217
Sal Celeski 222

Celilo Falls 21
Challis, Idaho 135
Chronology of the J. R. Simplot Company 92
Margaret Simplot Clayville 1, 3, 6, 10, 27
Mabel Coddington 152
College of Idaho xxii, 89, 113, 143, 155, 222
Colorado Women's College 155
Columbia River 21
Comptonville, California 141
Conda Mine 141, 174, 194
Conquest of Tuberculosis 13
Jim Conrad 165
Continental Illinois Bank 132
Burdell Curtis 71, 90

D

John Dahl 90, 114, 125, 128, 165, 166, 171
Hugo Dalsoglio 91
Bill Daniels 92
Cliff Darrington 67
Declo, Idaho 49, 78, 151
Declo—My Town, My People 29, 63, 67
Dehydrated Food Manufacturers of America 84
Desert Land Act 16
Diamond A Ranch 136
Dick Act 64
Rep. Charles W. Dick 64
Dominican Republic Central Bank 172
Downieville, California 94
Dubuque, Iowa 3, 4, 8, 11
George Duff 143
Ray Dunlap 90, 114, 118, 119, 122, 125
Dunlap-Kueneman Process 122
A. Dale Dunn 91, 171, 195, 196
Dale Dunn 167

E

Eighteenth Amendment 60
Ralph Waldo Emerson xxiii, 50
Environmental Protection Agency 196
Enyeart Hotel 47, 49, 79
Epworth, Iowa 7

F

Starr Farish 91
Farmers' Society of Equity 28
Forbes magazine 193
Fort Hall Indian Reservation 146
Fortune magazine xvii, 146, 193, 203, 210

G

Galena, Illinois 5
Florence Galvin 154
Gay Mine 154
Bill Gibson 69
George Gilder 168
Glenns Ferry, Idaho 77, 78
Grand Forks, North Dakota 174
Grand View Farms 94
Grand View 212
Greeley, Colorado 136
Milton Grosz 84
Grouse Creek Ranch 143, 147

H

Edward Everett Hale 170
Dr. William Webster Hall xxii
Halley's Comet 24
Paul Hansen 91
Harper's Weekly 3, 4
Harvest Hands 137
Cornelius Haxby 10, 22
Dorothy Bradley Haxby 98
Gale Haxby 62
Robert Haxby 21, 22
Clarence Hayden 62
Helm, California 194
Henry Phipps Foundation 159
Hermiston, Oregon 174, 194, 197
Heyburn, Idaho 141, 142, 194, 197
Homestead Act of 1862 16
Horseshoe Bend, Idaho 94
Hotel Baker 75
Howe Farms 142, 143

I

Idaho Falls, Idaho 71, 137
Idaho State Journal 145, 169
Idaho Statesman 176, 207, 212, 221, 222
Idaho Tri-Weekly Statesman 88
Institute of Food Technology 123
Iowa Beef 212
Iowa Iron Works 9
Iowa State Militia 4
Izmir, Turkey 194

J

J. R. Simplot Company 91, 130, 169, 176, 193, 201
J. R. Simplot Dehydrating Company 87, 126, 130
Jacksonville, Illinois 161
Judge Julian I. Jacobs 207
Jamieson Farms 94
Jamieson, Oregon 71
Jarbidge, Nevada 136
Leon Jones 90, 114, 125, 131, 165

K

Kellogg twins 75, 77
Frances Kellogg 76
Kendrick, Idaho 60
Keosauqua, Iowa 60
Grant Kilbourne xvi, 131, 143
King of the Hill 195, 203, 228
Klamath Falls, Oregon 136
Knipchild Manufacturing Company 86
Robert Koch 13
Ray Kroc xvii, 119, 123, 146
Ray Kueneman 90, 114, 119, 122, 124, 125
Kuna, Idaho 212

L

Hugh Larkin 92
Lathrop, California 194
Charles Le Clere 7
George Le Clere 2
Joseph Le Clere 1
Leeds, England 10
Lehi, Utah 205
Lincolnwood, Illinois 161
Colonel Paul P. Logan 84, 87
Bob Lothrop 92
J. Anthony Lucas 20

M

MacFries 146
MacMurray College 161
Lindsay Maggart 70, 109
Magma Copper Company 203
Manchester, England 6
McCall, Idaho 158
Ben McCollum 91, 171
Joe McCollum 91
McDonald's xvii, 124, 133, 146, 175, 214
Medford, Oregon 64
Herman Melville 218
Micron Technology 174, 176, 203, 208, 228
Milner Dam 19
Minidoka Project 19, 229
Model A Ford 61, 78
Moosejaw, Canada 68
Mormons 17, 28, 38, 195
Mountain Home, Idaho 21, 212
My Ántonia 217

N

National Defense Act of 1916 64
National Guard 64, 66
National Reclamation Act of 1902 19
Nauvoo, Illinois 3
Elizabeth Nelson 10, 97
Jane Nelson 10, 97
News Tribune 83
Tom Nicholson 175
Allen Noble 175
Ralph Nyblad 90
Nyssa, Oregon 143

O

O. E. Muir and Company 136
Ojai Prep School 153
Ojai, California 152
Carl Olsen 62, 63
Omro, Wisconsin 159
Ontario, Oregon 75
Oregon Trail 23
Oregonian 193
Origins of the J. R. Simplot Company 49
C. L. "Butch" Otter 155, 208
Overton, Nevada 135, 143, 193
R. C. Owens 153
Oxford Academy 153

P

Pacific Northwest Pollution Control Association 174, 196
The Palimpsest 3
Parish, New York 2
Joe Parkinson 203, 204
Ward Parkinson 175
Parma, Idaho 86
Pasco, Washington 212
Payette-Boise Project 20
Harriet Watts Pearson 6
Doug Pitman 175
Pocatello, Idaho xx, 67, 129, 131, 136, 137, 143, 166, 173, 174, 194, 222
Portable Lumber Company 135
potato sorter 70
Presque Isle, Maine 141

Q

Quartermaster Corps 125, 128

R

Steve Richardson 113, 132
David Riesman 49
Rock River Seminary 3
Rock Springs, Wyoming xx
John D. Rockefeller 48, 93, 117, 130, 144, 226, 227
Nelson Rockefeller 143, 171, 229
Rev. E. Rohn 223
Ruby Company Farms 147

S

"S-16" 205
Santa Rosa 35, 36
Saranac Lake, New York 14
Schenectady, New York 4
Andrew Serwer 203
Cliff Simons 71, 90
Simplot Aviation 147
Simplot Europe 194
Simplot Family Trust 203
Simplot Fertilizer Co. 89
Simplot Games 173
Simplot Hall 113
Simplot International 171, 194
Simplot Investment Co. 130
Simplot of Canada 142
Simplot Produce Co. 71, 87
Simplot Silica Products, Inc. 135
Simplot Soilbuilders xvii, 136, 143, 154, 165
Alexander Simplot 3
Charles Le Clere Simplot 4, 7
Charles Richard Simplot 4, 7, 8, 15, 21, 22, 28, 29, 35, 36, 37, 48, 65, 99, 100, 105, 106, 110, 112, 118, 132, 149, 150
Don John Simplot 150, 151, 152, 153, 155, 205, 208, 210
Dorothy Anne Simplot 34, 104, 105, 112
Dorothy Haxby Simplot 9, 10, 15, 22, 29, 35, 98, 99, 101, 110, 112, 149
Esther Becker Simplot xx, 159, 223
Ethel Lorraine Simplot 36, 105
Gay Corrine Simplot 113, 154, 158, 205, 208, 210
Henry Simplot 2
Jane Burton Simplot 7
John Richard "Jack" Simplot xv, xvii, xx, xxiv, 1, 2, 9, 10, 15, 21, 24, 28, 34, 35, 43, 44, 47, 49, 51, 54, 62, 65, 67, 75, 80, 83, 85, 92, 101, 102, 104, 105, 106, 107, 108, 109, 110, 111, 112, 117, 118, 123, 125, 134, 135, 138, 143, 151, 156, 157, 161, 167, 168, 169, 176, 193, 195, 201, 206, 212, 217, 219, 222, 225, 233, 235
Margaret Jane, "Peggy," Simplot 11, 35, 101, 102, 104, 106, 112
Mary Bonson Simplot 98
Mary Ellen Bonson Simplot 7
Myrtle Simplot 11, 35, 101, 102, 104
Richard Rosevear Simplot 150, 151, 152, 154, 155, 207
Robert LeRoy Simplot 32, 104, 105, 112

Ruby Rosevear Simplot 75, 77, 78, 111, 112, 113, 151, 156, 157, 158
Scott Robert Simplot 113, 156, 158, 175, 205, 208, 210
Susan Le Clere Simplot 3
Simplot-Devoe Lumber Company 135
Adam Smith 227
Gordon Smith 92, 167, 196, 210
Smoky Canyon Mine xx, 143, 194
Snake River 19
Snake River Valley 71, 83
Soda Springs, Idaho 141
Sokol and Company 84
John A. Sokol 84, 87
Southern Idaho College of Education 77
Springfield High School 67
St. Margaret's Hall 77, 78
Charlotte Stanford 152
A. K. Steunenberg 20
Frank Steunenberg 20

T

Taber, Alberta 147, 165
Texas Gulf Sulfur Company 143
The Great Valleys and Prairies of Nebraska and the Northwest 17
Greatest Show on Earth 34
The Lonely Crowd: A Study of the Changing American Character 45
The Small College Talks Back xxii
The Spirit of Enterprise 158
These Thousand Hills 45
Lowell Thomas xx, 173, 229
Three Creek Ranch 136
Tollman family 38
Marshall Tollman 107
Toppenish, Washington 143
Dr. Edward L. Trudeau 14
Trust Company in Chicago 132
Tulelake, California 143
Twin Falls Land and Water Company 19
Twin Falls 77, 154
Twin Peaks, Utah 143

U

U. S. Reclamation Service 19
Under the Lion's Paw 30
Union College 4
University of Idaho 156, 205
University of Leeds 10

V

Jean-Antone Villemin 13
Venice, California 34, 35
Vernal, Utah xx
The Virginian 45
Volstead Act 60

W

Selman A. Waksman's 13
Kate Maggart Walker 57
Hanry A. Wallace 20
Horace Walpole 3
Warren School 153
Washington School 35
Bob Whipkey xvi, 91
Walt Whitman 117, 149

Charles Dana Wilber 17
World War II 117

Y

Ron Yanke 175
Yellowstone Park 68, 203
Yorkshire 9, 10
Swaledale, Yorkshire 4

Z

Fred Zerza 211, 212, 221
ZX Ranch 210, 211

Other Books About Idaho From CAXTON PRESS

Snake River Country

ISBN 0-87004-215-7

12x15, 195 pages, cloth, boxed $39.95

River Tales of Idaho

ISBN 0-87004-378-1

6x9, 50 maps, 12 illustrations, 14 maps, 344 pages, paper

$17.95

A Cabin on Sawmill Creek

ISBN 0-87004-380-3

6x9, photographs, 228 pages, paper

$12.95

Gem Minerals of Idaho

ISBN 0-87004-228-9

6x9, 14 maps, 23 illustrations, 129 pages, paper

$18.95

Southern Idaho Ghost Towns

ISBN 0-87004-229-7

6x9, 14 maps, 95 illustrations, 135 pages, paper

$12.95

From the Ganges to the Snake River

An East Indian in the American West

ISBN 0-87004-397-8

6x9, 250 pages, paper

$14.95

Books to us never can or will be primarily articles of merchandise to be produced as cheaply as possible and to be sold like slabs of bacon or packages of cereal over the counter. If there is anything that is really worthwhile in this mad jumble we call the twentieth century, it should be books.

J. H. Gipson
Founder, Caxton Press, 1925

For a free Caxton catalog write to:

CAXTON PRESS
312 Main Street
Caldwell, ID 83605-3299

or

Visit our Internet Website:

www.caxtonprinters.com

Caxton Press is a division of The CAXTON PRINTERS, Ltd.

WC